Spiritual Warfare

Workbook 4

of the series,
Living a Supernatural Life, Naturally

by Linda Morgan

Spiritual Warfare

Workbook 4

of the series,
Living a Supernatural Life, Naturally

by Linda Morgan

Spiritual Warfare
by Linda Morgan
Part Four of the series, *Living a Supernatural Life, Naturally*

Copyright © 2022 Linda Morgan

All rights reserved. No part of this publication may be reproduced, distributed or transmitted in any form or by any means, or stored in a database or retrieval system without prior written permission of the publisher or author, except as allowed in brief review or article, with credit given to author, illustrator and publisher.

Print book ISBN: 978-1-954509-06-1

Scriptures marked HCSB are taken from the HOLMAN CHRISTIAN STANDARD BIBLE (HCSB): Scripture taken from the HOLMAN CHRISTIAN STANDARD BIBLE, copyright© 1999, 2000, 2002, 2003 by Holman Bible Publishers, Nashville Tennessee. All rights reserved.

Scriptures marked NIV are taken from the NEW INTERNATIONAL VERSION (NIV): Scripture taken from THE HOLY BIBLE, NEW INTERNATIONAL VERSION®. Copyright© 1973, 1978, 1984, 2011 by Biblica, Inc.™. Used by permission of Zondervan.

Scriptures marked ESV are taken from the THE HOLY BIBLE, ENGLISH STANDARD VERSION (ESV): Scriptures taken from THE HOLY BIBLE, ENGLISH STANDARD VERSION® Copyright© 2001 by Crossway, a publishing ministry of Good News Publishers. Used by permission.

Scriptures marked NKJV are taken from the NEW KING JAMES VERSION (NKJV): Scripture taken from the NEW KING JAMES VERSION®. Copyright© 1982 by Thomas Nelson, Inc. Used by permission. All rights reserved.

Quotations designated (NET) are from the NET Bible® copyright ©1996-2016 by Biblical Studies Press, L.L.C. http://netbible.com All rights reserved. Scripture quoted by permission. The names: THE NET BIBLE®, NEW ENGLISH TRANSLATION COPYRIGHT (c) 1996 BY BIBLICAL STUDIES PRESS, L.L.C. NET Bible® IS A REGISTERED TRADEMARK THE NET BIBLE® LOGO, SERVICE MARK COPYRIGHT (c) 1997 BY BIBLICAL STUDIES PRESS, L.L.C. ALL RIGHTS RESERVED

Illustration on page 71 © Drew Pryor. Used with permission.

Cover design by VisionRun.com
Photo credit: iStock

Printed in the United States
visionrun.com
For bulk orders, contact debbie@debbiepatrick.com

About the Author

Linda Morgan is a wife, mother, grandmother, business owner, and gifted Christian teacher. She is well known for her ability to express spiritual principles in everyday language. After being introduced to the person of the Holy Spirit in the 1970s, she has spent the years since then studying and sharing what she's learned with others.

She has ministered and taught in churches in the U.S., at retreats, through keynote addresses, and on mission trips to Europe and Central America. Linda has also had a personal prayer ministry for hurting people for over thirty years. She is passionate about helping others resolve inner and outer conflict through prayers that heal the heart and change lives.

As a business owner, she also consults and speaks to individuals and professionals alike on the importance of first impressions, and works with clients on wardrobe, color, style, and makeup.

Linda and her husband Dell make their home in Knoxville, Tennessee. They have been married since 1972 and have two grown children and seven grandchildren.

Table of Contents

About the Author 5

Introduction to the Series 9

Course Overview 11

Lesson 1: The Danger of Complacency 15

Lesson 2: The Enemy Targets Your Weaknesses 25

Lesson 3: Reality and Point of View 39

Lesson 4: Understanding the Triune Being of Man 49

Lesson 5: Good Guys vs. Bad Guys (Angels, Demons, and Us) 57

Lesson 6: Genuine Reality 67

Lesson 7: Demonization, Possession, and Oppression 81

Lesson 8: Understanding the Power of Evil Spirits 91

Lesson 9: Dangerous Open Doors 103

Lesson 10: Distinguishing Angels from Demons 123

Lesson 11: Align Your Will with God's 133

Lesson 12: Freedom 143

For Further Study 157

Appendix A: Breaking the Masonic Curse 159

Appendix B: Recognizing and Defining Demonic Activity 161

Appendix C: Angels, Demons, and Sons of God 169

Appendix D: Points of Note on Healing Prayer/Deliverance Ministry 173

Introduction to the Series, Living a Supernatural Life Naturally

For about thirty years prior to developing the material for this study, I had been involved in leading women's ministries. I sensed the Lord was telling me in 2011 that it was time for rest and recharging my spiritual batteries. It seemed He was telling me it was time to take care of myself physically and build up my spiritual man. I needed a time that involved *being* instead of *doing*.

So after pulling back from leading in our church for a season, I sensed the Lord saying it was time to get involved again. I began praying and asking Him what my purpose was now. It seemed He immediately spoke to my heart saying "I want you to teach a Bible Study in the fall. The title is *Living a Supernatural Life Naturally* and here are the ten topics." You can imagine that I immediately felt overwhelmed, but He reminded me that I had already taught most of those subjects over the years. So I've incorporated the ten into six workbooks: three topics in each of the first two, and four single-topic workbooks.

The purpose of this study is to bring an increased awareness, appreciation for, and understanding of the ministry of the Holy Spirit in our daily lives. The goal is to bring us deeper into His presence through the ministry of the Holy Spirit. We want to develop a listening ear that enables us to respond more readily to the still, quiet voice of the Spirit in our everyday lives.

We can know the Holy Spirit as a Person of the Godhead and not just think of Him as an impersonal influence in our lives. We want to begin to live supernaturally through the power of the Holy Spirit working in us to accomplish God's purposes by fully living the Christ life.

-Linda Morgan

Living a Supernatural Life Naturally: Course Overview

Christ delegated spiritual authority to believers; however, it's up to us to exercise that authority (2 Corinthians 10:3-5,8; Luke 9:1, 10:19, 19:17).

Workbook One: Grace, The Gift, and Living a Life of Faith

- **Grace** is not just God's favor; it is also His empowerment to us so that we can overcome our weakness and sin to do His will (Romans 6:14). Everyone who has grace has the Holy Spirit living in them and can live a supernatural life naturally. Jesus wants to live His life through us, as us.

- **The Gift** of the Holy Spirit was sent to us as a Helper. The Holy Spirit is a Person, not just an impersonal influence. Jesus did not leave us helpless (John 14:26, 15:26). Being filled with the Spirit is continual (Ephesians 5:18). Spiritual gifts are supernatural manifestations of God's power provided by the Holy Spirit.

- **Living a Life of Faith** - The gift of faith is like a mustard seed that must be planted, watered, fertilized, protected, and pruned. True spiritual life flows from our spirit and affects our mind. Faith is a gift of grace. Faith is taking that first step without seeing what is ahead. Faith occurs when we stop trying to do something by our own efforts and trust someone else to do it for us. Belief and faith are not the same. Acting on our belief means we have faith.

Workbook Two: Prayer, Listening, and Obedience

- **The Power of Prayer** happens when we believe that God is and that He rewards those who seek Him. Answered prayer affirms us (Hebrews 11:6). We pray because we believe (have faith) and hope that prayer changes things. Prayer is not overcoming God's reluctance but laying hold of His willingness.

- **Listening Prayer** - The Holy Spirit leads and guides us into all truth, but we have to develop a listening ear (John 16:13). God speaks to us both indirectly and directly; He is always speaking, but we are not always listening. God speaks to us and through us (1 Corinthians 12).

- **Obedience** - If we are willing and obedient, we will eat the good of the land (Isaiah 1:19). Obedience brings revelation (John 14:6). It is a key to destiny; it comes faster when we are obedient. Grace empowers us to live a life of obedience, and it empowers us to live beyond our abilities (John 21:15-17).

Living in the age of the New Testament means we are covered by grace and are under a new covenant. A covenant that means we don't have to work and struggle because we can rest in what Christ has provided. *We have the gift of the Holy Spirit, the very presence of Jesus living in us and enabling us to live a supernatural life, naturally.* It requires trusting that He is doing just that, and we don't have to make things happen. We pray, listen, and obey what the Spirit is saying. If we make a mistake and miss it (and sometimes we will), we confess, repent, and ask Him to empower us to do better. He has delegated spiritual authority to us, and when our hearts are right and our motives are pure, we can be effective over the enemy.

Workbook Three: Spiritual Authority

To defeat the enemy we must realize and believe we have been delegated authority in the spirit realm. The blood of Jesus and His resurrection defeats the enemy once and for all. We operate from a place of victory because He has already won and delegated His authority to believers. We have been given authority in the spirit realm, which enables us to win our battles in the natural realm too. This is how we live supernaturally, naturally.

Workbook Four: Spiritual Warfare

Spiritual warfare can sound violent or challenging, but it's actually neither. It's simply recognizing the enemy and defeating him through prayer, while using the Sword of the Spirit — the Word of God against him. We do need to understand Satan's strategy in order to know how to defeat him. To do that we must realize and believe we have been given authority in the spirit realm. We are more than conquerors (Romans 8:37; 1 John 4:4)!

Workbook Five: Healing Prayer

We often think of healing prayer as the gift of healing given by the Holy Spirit. This workbook, though, is about healing prayer that any Christian can use, either individually or in partnership with a few others to allow the Spirit to touch and begin to heal deeply wounded places in our hearts. Healing prayer is also a way to close the door to familial or familiar spirits and generational curses. It's a powerful tool to help find victory and healing to experience a more vibrant walk. In short, it's a path to emotional and spiritual healing.

Workbook Six: Destiny and Inheritance

Destiny involves recognizing God's plan for your life and overcoming obstacles to living it out. It requires learning to rest in the assurance that God has a special design for your life.

Lesson 1 – Danger of Complacency

Satan was banished from heaven.

You've probably heard of the Fall — when Adam and Eve sinned in the Garden of Eden and were banished from the idyllic place God had created for them. But did you realize this was the result of sin and rebellion in heaven? Most in Christian circles assume that the rebellion in heaven happened at some point before the Fall, but upon closer inspection of scripture, we are not sure about the timeframe; only that rebellion and sin happened, both in heaven and on earth.

Lucifer was created by God and scripture tells us he was full of wisdom and perfect in beauty; he was the "anointed cherub who covers." Many scholars believe he was part of the "council of God" (Psalms 82:1; 89:5-7). But he wasn't satisfied to be created and loved by God; he wanted to *be* God; he wanted to be worshipped. Ultimately, he led a rebellion against God and subverted other heavenly beings, fighting against the remaining heavenly host of angels, led by the archangel Michael. Lucifer and the fallen angels lost the battle, and were cast out of heaven. You can read about this in Revelation 12. Jesus also mentions it in Luke 10:18, "I saw Satan fall like lightning from heaven" (Ezekiel 28:12-17; Isaiah 14:12-17). While again, we don't know exactly *when* this happened, but we do know *that* it happened.

Knowing about this angelic rebellion helps give context to some of Jesus' actions. Hebrews 9:11-14, 23 explain first that the tabernacle Moses built here on earth is a copy of the original tabernacle in heaven. This section of Scripture goes on to explain that sin requires a *blood sacrifice* as payment. So Jesus the Messiah, our High Priest, entered the true, original Most Holy Place in heaven, cleansed it, and made final payment for our sins. Jesus then went into the lower parts of the earth and led the captives there back into the now cleansed heaven with Him (Ephesians 4:8-10; Psalm 68:18).

Revelation 12:10-12 tells us that since the salvation and the power and the kingdom of our God and the authority of His Messiah have now come, Satan has been thrown out. He was the one who "accuses [us] before our God day and night." Revelation 12:11 tells us that the saints conquered Satan by the blood of the [Jesus] and by the word of their testimony. It illustrates why our words are so important.

Discussion

Is there a time you can recall when someone's words affected you deeply?

Angels, demons, and spiritual warfare

Billy Graham, Tony Evans, and other pastors have told the story about a painting that used to hang in an art museum in Paris (it's now part of a private collection). The painting is called *Checkmate* and was painted by Friedrich Moritz August Retzsch in the late 1800s. It shows a young man playing chess with the devil. In the painting, the young man sits with sweat on his brow and a tear rolling down his cheek. Clearly, he is losing. As he looks hopelessly at the board, he doesn't see any way to win the game. The devil looks as if he can barely contain his excitement as he anticipates stealing the young man's soul as his prize. An angel stands between them, watching.

As the story is told, one day a chess champion came to the gallery. After carefully studying the painting until closing that day, he asked for a chessboard and set it up exactly as it was depicted in the painting. He began to play from there, taking turns for each side, making moves and counter moves, and keeping the devil's side on the defensive. He then showed the museum manager where the young man in the painting had miscalculated a very important move, but also how, even from his vulnerable position, he could have recovered. The chess champion not only discovered a way of escape for the young man in the painting, but he was also able to go on to checkmate the devil.

We can compare this battle of spiritual warfare to a chess game between God and Satan, where it may look at times like the devil is winning. Think about it. God makes the opening move by creating angels. Lucifer (the devil) counters by rebelling against God, taking one-third of the angels with him. God counters by creating mankind. Satan causes them to sin. Abraham is called to be father of a nation, holy and set aside as God's own. The devil arranges enslavement for them in Egypt. Move, counter move, all the way through the Old Testament.

Satan attacks God by attacking us. He hates humanity because we are made in God's image. But God's checkmate move is Jesus.

The blood of His death and resurrection defeats the devil once and for all. God wins, and we do as well because we are hidden with Christ in God (See Colossians 3:2-3). We operate *from* a place of victory because He has already won and delegated His authority to us as believers.

We have been given authority in the spirit realm, which enables us to win our battles in the natural realm too. This is how we live supernaturally, naturally.

 The point is, God always wins!

Satan's strategy has never changed.

The devil still preys on our weaknesses. Nothing has changed with Satan's plan or strategy. He still uses lies and deception to get his hook into us by promoting sins or openings to sin such as complacency, disobedience, deception, jealousy, willful sin, rebellion, worship of idols, and bondage.

Complacency and passivity led to disobedience.

Genesis 2:15-17 leads us to believe that Adam was told about the tree of knowledge of good and evil before Eve was created. It was to Adam that God said, "You shall not eat, [of that tree] for in that day that you eat of it you shall surely die." Then after those instructions in verse 18, God said he would make a helper fit for Adam. Eve was created in verses 21 and 22. So when Eve offered Adam the fruit of the forbidden tree, he knew exactly what it was, and what God had instructed. It seems that he chose Eve over God, and in his complacency he justified going along to get along. But then he blamed Eve when God called them both on their disobedience.

Discussion

Has complacency ever led you into sin, or to a place you really didn't want to be? What decisions did you make as a result of that experience?

1 Peter 5:8 tells Christians to be serious and alert because our adversary the devil is prowling around like a roaring lion, looking for anyone he can devour. When things are going well, we tend to become passive and complacent. Then we're easy prey for the enemy. (Adam's weakness was that he chose Eve over God.) If we're not on our guard, we are ripe for picking. God wants us to take the enemy seriously. Complacency will open the door to the enemy.

Eve, on the other hand, was ensnared by *deception*, which enabled Satan to take away the authority God had entrusted to her, along with Adam. This is one of his biggest weapons, and Christians are deceived in many areas. If he can't keep you from being a child of God, he will try to disarm you. He will try to steal your faith, or he will try to deceive you in ways that will keep you from maturing as a believer.

Jealousy is another tool the enemy uses to kill, steal, and destroy.

Cain murdered his brother Abel because of pride and jealousy. These twin emotions will sever human relationships, steal your peace, and destroy your witness. People do irrational things out of jealousy. It is fueled even more by the added weakness of insecurity.

Temptation into willful sin is the next tactic Satan uses against man.

Cain, driven by jealousy, willfully sinned when he murdered Abel. Most of us think we don't actually sin if we don't act on our wrongful thoughts and feelings, but God sees and cares about what is in our hearts. For example, scripture says if adultery (Matthew 5:28) is in our heart, we have committed the sin. In many scriptures, murder and adultery are listed together (Romans 13:9, see also Matthew 5:21, 15:19).

Willful sin begins with your thought life. Not all your thoughts originate with you.

When Satan's little "minion" assigned to you sees your weakness, he will use it to get his hook in, and lead you down the wrong path. While he's very good at the art of sinful suggestion, fortunately God gives us the ability to choose our path for ourselves; we have free will.

Discussion

Have you ever realized in the moment that thoughts you were having didn't originate with you? How does this differ from having angry thoughts that you don't act on, as warned about in Matthew 5:28?

After the Fall, sin and evil grew to the point that mankind was in total rebellion against God. Satan began to use pride along with jealousy, lust, lies, and anger in the minds and hearts of man to lead him to harm others easily and sin against God as if to do so was a "normal" part of the culture.

It is believed that Nimrod willfully sinned against God by introducing the worship of idols. He was the son of Cush and grandson of Noah (See Genesis 10). He was a violent man, described as a "mighty hunter" and a kingdom-builder, having built both the cities of Nineveh and Babel, located in Mesopotamia. The god Marduk was known to be over that region and is associated with Nimrod.

All of Satan's tools we've discussed: complacency, deception, idolatry, jealousy, pride, willful sin, and rebellion, lead to bondage. Israel became enslaved to Egypt because of rebellion against God's commandments. Nothing about that pattern has changed.

Willful sin and idolatry will cause us to be enslaved by the world's way of thinking.

Passively or actively going against what we know is God's will opens the door for the enemy to come into our lives and steal our identity, which is Satan's goal all along.

The work of the cross brings us back to the place God intended.

Discussion:

What are some ways Satan deceives believers?

Many Christians are deceived into participating in occult practices such as communicating with the dead, palm reading, psychics, and horoscopes. Because they don't know scripture, they don't realize that God forbids these practices. As a result, by indulging in these activities, believers open a door to Satan in their lives (Leviticus 19:31; Deuteronomy 18:9-14; Galatians 5:19-21).

Delegated Spiritual Authority

We have been given spiritual authority through Jesus to have victorious lives, not as controllers of our destinies, but as servants of God, carrying out and exercising our delegated authority over our divinely assigned projects.

Your delegated authority is within your sphere of influence: your family, your work, and your employees; if a pastor, it's your church; in government, it can be on the national or local level. There is temporal authority and spiritual authority. Pastors and elders have temporal authority in the church (1 Peter 5:1-5). Again, it is not about control, it's about prayer and speaking Truth. Where your children are concerned, your prayers are powerful (James 5:16). This is about speaking Truth into darkness.

Exercising authority requires a servant's heart of humility. Biblical authority goes vertical first, then horizontal to your sphere of influence. That is, we receive spiritual authority from Jesus (vertical), and we exercise that authority in our life and family through prayer (horizontal). Faith comes when we are living life under His authority and not under our own. (*For more about our delegated spiritual authority, see Workbook 3 in this series.*)

You can certainly pray for those outside your realm of family, but you have a unique authority when it is under your umbrella of spiritual covering. It also makes a difference to have others present *with* you, praying in agreement, as well as praying *for* you. See Leviticus 26:8, which says 5 can chase a 100, and 100 puts 10,000 to flight; your enemies will fall before you, so we know there is strength in numbers, especially when it comes to spiritual support.

In applying this today, it tells us that we need a faith-based support group. This means for many of God's assignments, it takes a group effort; we simply can't do it alone. We need help to rebuild the walls, as Nehemiah did, be they literal or figurative. Interesting tidbit: archeologists have discovered remnants of the walls Nehemiah rebuilt and they were eight feet thick! That's the kind of spiritual support we build when we support each others' efforts in prayer.

Incidentally, the pattern used against Nehemiah is the one most often used by the evil one in trying to stop our plans: ridicule first, followed by attempts to twist the law, escalating finally to threats of violence. Today we still see him use intimidation, manipulation, and finally domination.

Discussion

Have you ever used the power of a group praying about a situation to resolve it? Share what happened.

His mercies are new every morning.

In scripture, eight is the number symbolizing new beginnings. For example, after the seven days of creation, the eighth day was a new beginning for planet earth and mankind. On the eighth day, Hebrew boys were circumcised, which foreshadowed and symbolized a new, circumcised heart for each believer at salvation. God will always give us a fresh start when we confess, repent, and forgive (Colossians 2:11).

Lesson 1: The Danger of Complacency

As important as it is to have a community of spiritual support, it is even more important to build and sustain your personal relationship with God.

A spiritual exercise, such as the following, will be at the end of each lesson, to help you develop a deeper understanding of grace and hearing the voice of the Holy Spirit.

 **God Moment:**

Close your eyes and listen…

Beloved, come away with Me to a quiet place. Get still and focus on My love for you and all that is yours through the cross. There is nothing you can do to make Me love you more. You are not lacking in anything.

Come away and sit with Me. Let Me pour water over you from My well that never runs dry. I want to soothe away your tiredness, strengthen your bones, and breathe life back into you. I'm calling you deeper.

Song of Solomon 2:10
Mark 6:31
John 4:10

Assignment:

Ask God to show you some areas where you are deceived and list them.

_____

_____

What are some idols in your life?

_____

_____

Have you ever knowingly sinned, and if so, how did that affect you?

_____

_____

What does exercising authority in prayer look like for you?

_____

_____

Final thought:

Spiritual authority begins vertically then extends horizontally.

Lesson 2 — The Enemy Targets Your Weaknesses

More lessons from Nehemiah

Satan will use *fear and intimidation* to keep us from God's will. We see an example of this happening when God called Ezra and Nehemiah to rebuild the Temple walls. It starts in Nehemiah 1 with an afflicted and disgraced remnant of Israelites. When they saw the gates were broken down and the walls of their homeland were destroyed by fire, they were ashamed.

Shame often reflects our spiritual condition. When our spiritual walls against the enemy are broken down and our conscience is seared by sin, we become too ashamed to admit we need help. We fear being rejected and judged by our peers if we admit our weaknesses.

The first thing Nehemiah did was to confess, repent, and intercede on behalf of the nation. When we do the same, the Lord will not condemn us; He will comfort and restore us.

Nehemiah had a trusted position with the king as his cupbearer. (A cupbearer would draw off some of the liquid and pour it into his left hand to swallow it to be sure it wasn't poisoned.)

Even so, Nehemiah was afraid to be transparent and honest with the king about what was in his heart causing his sadness. When he stopped pretending and admitted to the king that something was wrong, the king awarded him with the authority, resources, and time off to go and restore the walls. The king delegated authority to Nehemiah that encompassed others. Likewise, our King has delegated authority to us to impact the kingdom of darkness, especially on behalf of others.

God knows our hearts even better than we do, and He knows our struggles, especially when our lives are in ruins. These feelings of unease could represent damage to our spiritual walls and be telling us our defense against sin has been torn down, that we have allowed the enemy to come in to steal, kill, and destroy our lives and relationships through sin.

Think of your five senses like personal gates. Gates are important places in the Bible. The elders met there to make important decisions that affected many lives. Our personal gates include our mouth, tongue, ears, eyes, and hands as well as our thoughts/minds. They remind us that we should be careful what we look at, read, hear, say, touch, and think.

Just as Nehemiah used wisdom in what he said and to whom he spoke about what he was doing, we need to have wisdom about what we see, hear, say, and dwell on. We can give the enemy too much information and allow him to gain a foothold. Nehemiah waited for the right timing for others to stand with him.

Discussion

Have you ever been hesitant to go to God with your true feelings? What happened?

When God convicts us and we confess and repent, He will comfort us in the midst of our personal shortcomings to reassure us that He still loves us. He will give you the desires of your heart. Then when you receive healing and encouragement, you can encourage others. Nehemiah means "Yahweh comforts" (2 Corinthians 7:13; Ephesians 6:22).

When Nehemiah told the king why he was so sad, the king asked him to be specific about what he wanted. When we pray about something, we also need to be specific with the Lord about exactly what we are asking Him to do.

As a result, in Nehemiah 2 the King sends an army with Nehemiah. When we become honest about our struggles and repent of our sin, God will send an army of warring angels to fight our battle for us. Nehemiah prayed for four months before asking for help; after that he wasn't alone. We cannot be effective in winning our battles without others and without God's help. However, Nehemiah used wisdom regarding whom he told about what he was doing.

In Nehemiah 2:10, 4:1-5 Sanballat heard the Jews were rebuilding the walls and became furious. He didn't like it that someone had come to seek the welfare of the people of Israel. The enemy won't like it either when we begin to exercise spiritual authority and try to get free and help others experience freedom.

Satan used Sanballat to begin attacking the Jews with ridicule and tried to cause confusion. He mocked them and called them feeble. Satan will counter attack when you start receiving Truth and getting free.

Nehemiah 6:9 says, *They all wanted to frighten them thinking 'their hands will drop from the work and it will not be done.' But now, O God, strengthen my hands.* The key in exercising spiritual authority and engaging in spiritual warfare is to know that God will fight your battle, but you also have to act on what you believe God is telling you to do. You may not think you are powerful enough to defeat the enemy, but God will honor your efforts.

Sanballat tried to intimidate them. Mocking is ridicule's power based on peer pressure. It will possibly be by those you have respected and looked up to in the past. The enemy will not like it when you try to live victoriously, so he will set you up to be ridiculed by someone whose opinion matters to you to put you back in bondage.

The enemy sent an important person in the community, Shemaiah, to tell Nehemiah they were coming to kill him and tried to get him to hide in the temple. Nehemiah realized the enemy was trying to get him to take matters into his own hands to save himself instead of relying on God. If you look at it in the natural it would seem the right (religious) thing to do – to hide in the temple. But if Nehemiah was a eunuch (which is likely, given his position in the king's court), he was forbidden to enter the temple, so the enemy wanted to tempt him to sin. He understood that the enemy wanted to intimidate him using prophetic people, whom he should have been able to respect and trust.

It says in verse 8 that they conspired to come and attack Jerusalem and cause confusion. This is a good example of how the demonic realm will try to confuse you by making you doubt you are really healed or free. The enemy will put someone in your path to make you doubt your experience was real. He will also make you think you are not strong enough to walk it out and try to make you think that Christ in you isn't enough. *He wants to steal your faith.*

Discussion

Have you ever experienced a time when you knew you needed to stand firm in the face of mockery or ridicule, or of an authority figure's misdirection?

In Nehemiah 6:16 it says that when their enemies heard the work was finished, the nations around them were afraid and knew it had been accomplished with the help of their God. When others see that God has done for us what we couldn't, it glorifies Him and makes the enemy afraid. Once our confidence is in the Lord and not our own strength, he fears what we can accomplish. God's grace is all we need to overcome.

Another strategy Satan uses is superstition and legalism.

Superstition and legalism are actually opposite ends of the same spectrum. Superstition is when we try to manipulate our circumstances by what we do. Legalism is when we try to manipulate God by what we do. It's all still fear based (2 Timothy 1:7).

Legalism tries to gain favor with God in the realm of the supernatural. It's trying to appear holy to God and to those we want to impress. We think, "*if I do this, then God will bless me with that …*"

Superstition is when we try to bring good luck in the natural realm by what we do. "*If I do this a certain way, things will go well, and I'll have good fortune. If I don't follow the pattern, something bad will happen.*"

Both can dominate our behavior. Satan is laughing because he has taken away grace in our lives and stolen our peace and joy. Look at the fruit and you will recognize the enemy's strategy.

Sometimes people want a quick fix to their problems but are not willing to do what's needed in order to be free. This often goes back to an underlying superstition, or tendency to be legalistic.

Examples of legalism and superstition:
- Thinking you have to pray the same prayer in the same situation to get the same results [*superstition*]
- Wearing medals of saints for protection [*superstition*]
- People in sports tend who think what they wear or do before or during a game will influence the outcome [*superstition*]

- Not being able to make any decision without first praying and or fasting about it [*legalism*]
- Using objects that are symbols of good luck to get what you are hoping for (The Egyptian ankh is a cross with a loop at the top representing a sex goddess who despises virginity. It's a symbol for promoting fertility rites, worshiping Ra, the sun god, which is the same as worshipping Lucifer) [*superstition*]
- Thinking that you have to perform in order to have favor with God [*legalism*]

Wrong beliefs.

The Israelite remnant had to have a right attitude of belief along with the right actions. When you don't, when you agree with the enemy, your emotions will follow and your body will be affected. Your walls that keep the enemy out will start to crumble. Remember, the walls we're talking about here are healthy walls, built through faith, obedience, and right relationship with God.

Nehemiah 4:6 says, "They had a mind to work." Your mind affects your brain, and your body follows.

Group discussion:

How do superstition and legalism steal your peace and joy, and how do they appear to affect grace?

Another strategy Satan uses is judging.

When people judge others it puts them in a deeper prison. There is a truth that sets people free and there is a truth that binds people up through condemnation. One produces life, the other death. The truth of God's love and how He sees us brings freedom from the lies we have been imprisoned by. Speaking the truth to someone in a "black and white," legalistic, or judgmental way brings bondage. There is a time to pray, and then there will come a time to speak the truth in love in a way that brings freedom.

Many times we judge people based on a critical or suspicious spirit. This can result in bitterness, anger, or even self-pity at being a victim of it all. Our suspicions may cause us to think we are operating in the gift of discernment, but the gift is discerning of spirits, not discernment which may just be coming from a suspicious spirit.

Self-pity: We fall into temptation because we think we deserve something we didn't get in the past or that we don't have now. We think others have it better than us. We begin to obsess over what we think is unfair in life and imagine how much better others have it. We begin to compare ourselves to and envy people we think have had a better life or seem to have it all now. We begin to blame others for our situation and circumstances in life. We get resentful or angry with God for allowing it, which leads to an offense, so we start thinking, *"Why not? I deserve whatever makes me happy."*

This pattern leads pretty quickly into sin and bondage. Author Tim Keller said, "Satan shows us the bait but hides the hook so we only look at short-term pleasure."

If you identify with any of the above, with the help of your prayer warriors you can pick up the pieces and quickly start putting them back in place. But you need someone watching your back because that is the one place not protected. When you run from Satan, your back is exposed. The enemy is sneaky and will come in the back door or window after you have closed off the front entrances. Ask God to show you any vulnerable places.

In Nehemiah they built the walls while holding a sword in one hand. The sword we use is the Word of God; it's the only offensive weapon listed in Ephesians 6. Find the scriptures that apply to your situation and speak them out of your mouth as often as needed — every time the enemy attacks your mind with doubt, fear, intimidation, accusations, etc.

Another of Satan's strategies is to gain control when we don't take our thoughts captive.

Satan can't read our minds, but he can observe our behavior and infer quite a bit. He can also insert thoughts into our minds. We make it easier when we don't take charge of our thoughts.

We counter his attacks on our thoughts by making different choices in response (2 Corinthians 10:3-5). Believe that all things will work for your good (Romans 8:28).

An example of warfare involving your mind and thoughts could be when Satan brings up something from the past and starts firing darts of guilt, condemnation, and shame. You can choose to use the shield of faith not to accept his attack. Otherwise, you'll end up going down a path like this: You start agreeing with the thoughts such as: *yes, I'm a shameful, dirty sinner who has no hope of ever changing; people wouldn't like or accept me if they knew my past and the things I've done. Of course with a past like mine God cannot possibly want to use me.*

An example of warfare involving emotions would happen when you begin to be depressed because condemnation offers no hope. (When God brings conviction, He always offers hope.) You will lack self-confidence. Panic attacks can begin to manifest and self-pity soon follows as a result of believing you are stuck in the past, especially if abuse was involved.

An example of warfare involving your behavior happens when you adopt a victim mentality, which can make you resentful, untrusting, suspicious of others, etc. It also occurs if you feel shame, which can keep you from being open and transparent, hindering your ability to be free from your past. It can cause you to isolate.

💚 In all of these instances, you will not experience real community because you will be afraid of letting people get close.

Examples of spiritual warfare involving the hindrance of spiritual growth include not being able to move past your circumstances because you are chained to your past, usually through unforgiveness. Or, you have difficulty experiencing real intimacy with God because you need a revelation of His grace, love, and forgiveness. In this case, you don't grow spiritually because you don't feel worthy of being more than *you think* you are, instead of embracing who *God says* you are.

Wrong beliefs can be fueled by legalism and superstition. Your wrong beliefs might be things like:

1) You think God is punishing you for something in your past.

2) You are struggling with sin, and think that means you must not be saved.

3) You think God has favorites and you're not one.

4) You think things will never be different.

5) You think God isn't pleased because you're not doing enough in a certain area of life.

6) You think there must be something wrong with you, or that you're flawed or inadequate in some way.

💚 We need a revelation of Grace to counter wrong beliefs.

Discussion:

What are some of our wrong beliefs?

💚 When we're stuck in warfare, a revelation of what Christ has done for us brings victorious living: We have a new identity; we are more than conquerors (Romans 8:37-39).

We are already victorious; in fact, we now rule and reign with Christ because He is seated at the right hand of God. We are His body implementing His will on earth, using the authority over darkness He has delegated to us as believers (Mark 16:19; Hebrews 1:3; 1 Peter 3:22).

Even though he is a defeated foe, the enemy still tries to deceive us. Today we see the battle continue to escalate through mystical religions, psychics, mediums, New Age, fantasy roleplaying games, movies, etc. as they have all become "mainstream" and accepted as "normal." This is largely due to the fact that the Church has lost its sense of spiritual power, which, if recovered, would enable her to cope with this rise in demonic activity.

It works like this: If we don't understand that we have been delegated spiritual authority over this supernatural realm, we will not want to nor be able to stand against the wiles of the devil.

In Lesson 1 we looked at how Adam's complacency led him to sin rather than stand strong. We can become complacent too, where the enemy is concerned. And like Adam, that complacency can cost us dearly. We must use everything in our (God-given) power to regain the victorious life Christ intended.

As a nation, we have been desensitized by evil spiritual schemes behind the world's agenda, which have taken control and caused us to accept issues such as sexual perversion, pornography, greed, lust, occult activity, adultery, and idolatry as "normal" and perfectly okay. The spiritual element behind these issues can't be underestimated, as evil saturates the culture and deceives good people.

Remember that our battle is with the spiritual beings inspiring these attitudes and behaviors. (You may have heard the admonition to "love the sinner, hate the sin.")

As you deal with the effects of a fallen world within your delegated domain, remember that Satan doesn't use logic; therefore, you can't reason with a demon, but you can reason with the person the demon in influencing. When praying for someone, we need intuition and discernment to know if we are dealing with demonically-dominated behavior. We also need the ability to reason with the person. Therefore, both intuition and reason need to be Spirit-led.

Discussion:

Have you ever felt as if you were making no progress when trying to reason with someone? Do you think there could have been some demonic influence? Explain.

God Moment:

Close your eyes and picture…

See the Lord with open arms waiting for you to come into His embrace. Go to Him like a little child. Tell Him how much you love and adore Him. Wrap your arms around His neck and give Him a hug and call Him Abba Father.

If you don't feel comfortable doing that, ask Him why not and listen. Journal what you believe He is saying to you.

If you don't love Him like that, admit it and ask Him to help you love Him that way.

Psalms 131:2

Luke 18:17

Assignment:

How has legalism affected your spiritual life?

_____

_____

_____

How have you been superstitious?

_____

_____

_____

List some ways your thinking needs to change

_____

_____

_____

Final Thought:

Whatever controls your mind controls your actions. Our will overrides the work of the enemy when we receive the Truth.

Journal:

Lesson 3 — Reality and Point of View

As we mentioned in Lesson 1, Spiritual Warfare has been a part of the human experience since Genesis 3. To deal with this today, we need to 1) first ask God for a new perspective and understanding of the natural and supernatural realm; 2) we need to examine our worldview, rooting out places where other-than-God's belief systems have crept into and influenced our own, and finally, 3) acknowledge the reality of spiritual warfare and be willing to deal with it. Let's take these issues one by one.

Worldview

In our typical Western culture there's a real problem with finding a place for spiritual warfare to exist. This is because we (as a culture) have developed a worldview that believes in a complete dichotomy between science on one hand and religion on the other. It's been called the mystification of religion and the secularization of science, when in fact, God is the author of both our faith (religion) and our world (science), and they are an integrated whole in all of His creation.

The separation of religion and science results in believing spirits or spirit activity is exclusive to the supernatural realm. There is no acknowledgement that the supernatural can affect the natural. We have not been taught that the invisible spiritual realm has a definite effect on the natural realm.

The Cost of Not Knowing

Years ago someone who was close to me had an obsessive-compulsive disorder. They dealt with the outward manifestations through psychology, but it turned out that there was a spiritual root that opened the door, that was still present and had manifested in other ways over time. This person was later set free from all the manifestations caused by the demons when the evil spirits were cast out. (This is done through healing prayer, which usually involves deliverance. This is covered in-depth in the next Workbook in this series.)

Unfortunately, had we understood the demonic influence earlier, this person could have lived a very different life. Not seeing and acting on the spiritual truth of the situation cost them relationships, and affected their relationship with God. Many times people need spiritual help first, then counseling so they can learn to make better choices. Conversely, if you have a common issue that is not being helped through traditional means — investigate the possiblity of a spiritual root.

The Western worldview assumes that for any phenomenon in the human life or the physical world, there has to be a scientific explanation, or it simply "isn't real."

Spirits, if recognized at all, are seldom thought to invade the human experience. For example, no one considers whether or not a problem is spiritual or psychological. We never even look for causes in the spiritual realm that might be affecting the natural realm.

If we can step outside of our upbringing for a moment, we should immediately see the fallacy inherent in this point of view.

As Christians, we know God spoke the world into existence and performed miracles throughout the Old and New Testaments. Jesus said God was looking for worshippers to worship (believe) in Spirit and in Truth (John 4:23-24). That sounds like a fully integrated physical and spiritual world. Ask God to open your spiritual eyes on your understanding of these two dimensions.

Clearly, our popular Western worldview was foreign to those in Biblical times, and still is in much of the world today. Many cultures view life quite differently. That is why it is so easy for the Holy Spirit to manifest in other countries to bring healing and miracles; they expect the supernatural. That is also why, as early as Augustine, some parts of the Bible were changed to align with current thinking, rather than reflecting what the ancient writings said. An example would be "sons of God" in Genesis 6:1-4 being taught as referencing humans vs. supernatural beings. The original language clearly refers to giants that were a hybrid race, offspring between spiritual and human beings. This thinking is supported in 2 Peter 2:4-10 and Jude v. 6.

Other countries' cultures have their own spiritual pitfalls too. Syncretism in particular is one to be wary of. It is the fusion of all (or many) different forms of belief. Animism is another popular belief outside of Western culture — the belief that all natural and inanimate objects have souls or spirits on an equal level with mankind. This makes man just another element of nature, rather than a special being created in the image of God.

It has been said that seeing is believing, when in practice, the opposite is more often true — believing a certain thing causes (or at least influences) what one sees. Consider how the same evidence is used in a courtroom by both sides to "prove" either guilt or innocence, depending on what the attorneys can make the jury believe about what they see.

People with animistic beliefs see spirits as involved with all aspects of life, whereas our Western culture thinks it is superstition or ignorance to think that spirits could be involved in our lives at all. So both groups are "seeing" what they already believe.

Their impoverished theologies don't answer their ultimate questions of life, death, and eternity. Our science alone can't answer all the events of everyday life. The truth is, some experiences in the natural have natural causes, while others are rooted in the supernatural realm.

Evil spirits are real, and no scientific explanation is going to make them go away. But without being shown the power of Christ, people under oppression, whether by demonic or circumstantial origin, will resort to the practices they know. The worldviews we've been discussing, often labeled "Eastern" or "Western" worldviews, are no longer limited in their geography. For example, in Miami, there is a group of people who practice "Santeria," where they sacrifice animals to saints (demon spirits) in voodoo rituals.

Today's Western worldview-based Church in America practices a form of syncretism when we don't believe in spirits in general, nor do we acknowledge that spirits have any ability to affect our human/material world even though there are examples of spiritual influence over life throughout scripture. Spiritual realities are simply incompatible with our so-called technologically advanced society. We think we have to reason out everything and have an intellectual answer for it. This is actually secularism, and it shuts down the entire spiritual realm of life. Ignoring major aspects of life doesn't make them go away, but it certainly doesn't provide good ground for spiritual growth either. (See Timothy Warner's book, *Spiritual Warfare* for more on this subject.)

No worldview is thoroughly Christian until it includes a functional belief in the existence and activity of angels and demons.

We say we believe the entire Bible, but when we don't understand a part of it, we often choose to ignore that part. The problem is we don't think it applies to us, or even still exists in our modern society, much less that it has any influence over us as Christians. We don't realize how important it is to us and how much it does affect our everyday lives.

Discussion:

If you believe that spirits have any ability to affect our human/material world, what do you think that looks like?

Our true worldviews are held at a subconscious level. We may say we believe a certain set of realities, but our actions betray our real, true beliefs. An old cliche notes that, "People may not live what they profess, but they will always live what they believe." Our worldview is what we really believe, and if we embrace the whole scripture, we have to believe that demons exist.

> *There was a guy from Carson Newman College in the early '70s who came to our very liberal Baptist church and scientifically explained away demons, healings, and miracles in the Bible from an intellectual point of view. As a young adult in my late twenties, I thought it was very modern thinking. It portrays the people in biblical times as being ignorant of the real causes of problems, so Jesus used the term demons because that was what they could relate to. But it also implies that the God who created us didn't recognize the difference between spiritual and psychological problems, and refused to "tell it like it is."*

Do you see the arrogance in his teaching? The syncretism, merging our logic with scripture, as if God dumbed down His message, but now we know better than God?

If we believe the Bible over man's "filter," we know that spiritual warfare is real. Satan was originally one of the highest Cherubim and possibly a "guardian angel." We see Cherubim pictured on earth covering the Mercy Seat in the Tabernacle. This is a picture of the throne of God. We don't know if Satan was represented by one of those, but he clearly had a very trusted position with direct access to God. He was beautiful and powerful and must have had one of the highest ranks in heaven. Satan was not created as evil; he made a conscious immoral choice and became evil as a result (Ezekiel 28:14). It wasn't enough to guard and reflect the glory of God. Satan became jealous of God and wanted glory and worship for himself. He instituted idolatry and even tried to get Jesus to worship him (Matthew 4:9).

Understanding God's Cosmic Order

Genesis 3:22-23 says that man had become like one of "them" and now knew evil and had to be put out of the Garden before they ate of the Tree of Life and became immortal. Is the phrase "one of them" referring to more in addition to the Trinity, such as the "sons of God" who were members of the divine council mentioned in other places?[1]

Discussion:

What was Genesis 3:22-23 talking about? Was this referring to the Sons of God that were part of God's supernatural family?

Evil began with the fall of Satan because of his desire to put his throne before God's and receive God's glory.

Perhaps Satan's domain was literally in Eden as described in Ezekiel 28:12-16 before the Fall. I don't think these verses are just talking about an earthly king ruling in the natural realm. I think God is talking about the demonic principality operating through the human king.

Verse 12 says, *"You were the seal of perfection, full of wisdom and perfect in beauty."* A seal was a royal stamp made by the king's signet ring. It was sometimes made from semi-precious stones. It

---

[1] For more information on the sons of God, see *The Unseen Realm*, by Michael Heiser.

represented authority, and in this instance, perfection and beauty. This entity was also full of wisdom.

In verse 13 it says he was in Eden, the Garden of God. It says he was covered in every kind of precious stone. The mountings and setting were crafted in gold. Gold represents deity. This obviously is talking about a supernatural being in addition to a human kind and reminds us of the precious stones on the high priest's breastplate representing the tribes of Israel. The priests of Israel were supposed to intercede and protect the people of God. They wore them over their hearts so when they entered the Holy Place they symbolically carried the tribes in with them.

Satan no longer has any influence or authority on God's holy mountain (see verse 14; mountains and gardens are where the ancients believed gods lived), but he still supernaturally controls earth's atmosphere, which manifests in the natural realm. The Bible is full of symbolism, which is revealing Truth. So this is a case of "both/and" rather than "either/or." Satan's lofty place of ruling man is in our minds – lofty opinions or high-minded things, everything that exalts itself against the knowledge of God (2 Corinthians 10:3-5).

Isaiah 2:2 says that in the latter days the mountain of the Lord's house will be established at the top of the mountains and will be raised up above the hills. All nations will stream to it.

The fruit of Adam and Eve's disobedience was death, even though they'd been designed to live forever. Now they were mortal, and the immediate result of their sin was shame, blame shifting (each one not wanting to own what they had done), jealousy, lying, murder, idolatry, and more.

We need to examine our fruit each day to see where it is rooted: life or death. Things in the natural realm have roots in the supernatural realm. When we are struggling with something, we should look at the fruit and ask God to show us how the root formed and how to pull it up. Which tree is it rooted in, life or death?

We are called to live in the world, but not be of the world. All the works of the flesh can be countered with the Word of God. This is easier to put in practice when we know our identity in Christ.

Galatians 5:19-22 Fruit of the Spirit	Galatians 5:19-22 Fruit of fall: works of the flesh
Love	Hatred, strife, jealousy, envy
Joy	Dissensions, factions
Peace, Patience	Drunkenness
Kindness	Anger
Goodness	Sexual immorality
Faith	Idolatry, sorcery
Gentleness	Moral impurity
Self control	Carousing

Discussion:

How do we offer bad fruit to those around us? Could one example be by not loving them enough to care?

Disobedience will affect your influence, prayer life, worship, and devotion; it will take away your joy, your power over the enemy, and commitment to your calling, which affects your legacy. The battle is for your mind, even in seemingly "good" things (1 Timothy 6:6-12).

Discussion:

Has anyone ever said or done something that triggered an unresolved issue in you? What happened? Describe your reaction, and ask God where this reaction could be rooted in your past.

God Moment:

Close your eyes and picture…

You are in the midst of a garden and surrounded by beautiful flowers of every color. The fragrance is like nothing you have ever experienced. Now listen and hear the Lord say:

My beloved, you delight Me the same way these flowers delight you. Your fragrance is pleasing to others and Me as you allow My love to flow through you to those I bring into your life.

When you need refreshing, come back into My presence and feel My pleasure as you rest in this garden I have prepared for you. Then you will have something to offer those who cross your path needing beauty for ashes and a different aroma.

As I supply your needs, you will supply the needs of others.

Ephesians 5:2

Philippians 4:18

Isaiah 61:3

Assignment:

Describe a time when causes in the spiritual realm might have been affecting the natural realm.

_____
_____
_____

What has been your worldview? Has it changed? If so, in what ways?

_____
_____
_____

Would it be scary for you to believe that demons exist? Why or why not?

_____
_____
_____

Final thought:

Remember that people may not live what they profess, but they will always live what they believe.

Lesson 4 — Understanding the Triune Being of Man

Man is spirit, soul, and body.

Scripture says we are spirit, soul, and body (1 Thessalonians 5:23). We have a renewed spirit when our spirit is joined to the Holy Spirit at the new birth, and that's where Christ is formed in us (this is why I don't believe the spirit and soul are one and the same). In the realm of the soul, the mind has to be renewed because that is where Satan wants to set up a throne to dominate and influence our thinking and decisions, which in turn our body will execute. Our emotions will agree with whatever is dominating us. However, our will overrides the work of the enemy when we receive the Truth and obey it.

It is hard for some people to receive the things of the Spirit, the supernatural things of God, because of their intellect. We think this is just an analytical problem, but if they are intellectuals, it can actually be a spirit of "academia," similar to "a carnal mind" that is hindering them. The spirits attached to that stronghold are usually rooted in pride and self-rule. Their emotions might be shut down, and they still think they can "do it themselves."

Satan doesn't own us because we belong to God, but if he can dominate our thinking and behavior, he will in effect control us through patterns of wrong thinking. He will deceive and manipulate us into doing his will.

We are made in the image of God and were made to rule over our spiritual and physical world even though we are mortal beings. One way we experience this is when we take our thoughts captive and don't allow our emotions to dictate our actions. We allow the

Holy Spirit to rule through us, but this doesn't mean we rule over people. It's up to each individual to walk in his/her new freedom.

The Holy Spirit communicates mysteries of God to our spirit.

Once we receive salvation, we have a spirit connection to the heart of God that reveals to us the deep things of God. Before receiving a new spirit the disciples argued with each other, were fearful, and scattered. Peter even denied Christ three times. After the Holy Spirit came on the Day of Pentecost, Peter and all of the disciples were bold witnesses for Jesus, and most were even martyred for the sake of the gospel.

Discussion

How have you changed since receiving Christ as Lord of your life? Read Psalm 8:5. If you believe this is true, how will it change how you live your life?

Each person has a spirit encased within a soul. The longer people resist yielding to the Holy Spirit, the more influence the soul has, which can keep them from hearing God. The continued resistance enables the wall against God to become stronger, making it harder for the Spirit to convict and penetrate their hardened heart.

Look at the illustration and imagine the outer circle represents our whole body, the inner circle surrounded by a wall represents the soul, and inside the soul, an egg represents your spirit. The thickness of the wall depends on the hardness of your heart. Next, picture the lightning of God striking at the instant of salvation and charging your spirit with the Spirit of God, represented by the heart.

After salvation your spirit is like a fertilized egg. A new life begins. It needed the "Son" to fertilize it. When you respond to

God's invitation to new life in Him, the seed of salvation is called being born again. You then water your new life with God's Word.

The Seed of heaven enters our spirit and new life begins. The Holy Spirit lives in you to the extent that you remove the limitations.

The body will follow the dictates of the soul. The soul includes the mind, which is the intellectual power of the brain; it includes wisdom, knowledge, and reasoning. The brain relates to the mind and the body because it is the control center for both. The will is the volitional power to choose, and it controls thought processes of the brain. Your heart is the bridge between the soul and the spirit. The spirit is where we have communion with God through worship.

When a person becomes born again, the Holy Spirit becomes one with the human spirit, enabling the conscience to become the voice of the Holy Spirit. Intuition involves the spiritual senses, not the soul or physical senses. It is a direct sensing with no outside influence from the mind or emotions. It's a "knowing" through intuition while the mind helps us understand.

For a believer, intuition or perception should be from the Holy Spirit. But non-believers can be easily deceived into practicing ESP (Extra Sensory Perception). As a believer, the body should follow the dictates of the spirit under the direction of the Holy Spirit, not the soul, which is influenced by the flesh. The enemy plants thoughts in our minds to deceive us, but the Holy Spirit will guide us into all Truth.

Discussion:

How do we limit the Holy Spirit?

A Biblical Picture of Man
Man — A Three-Part Whole
(I Thessalonians 5:23)

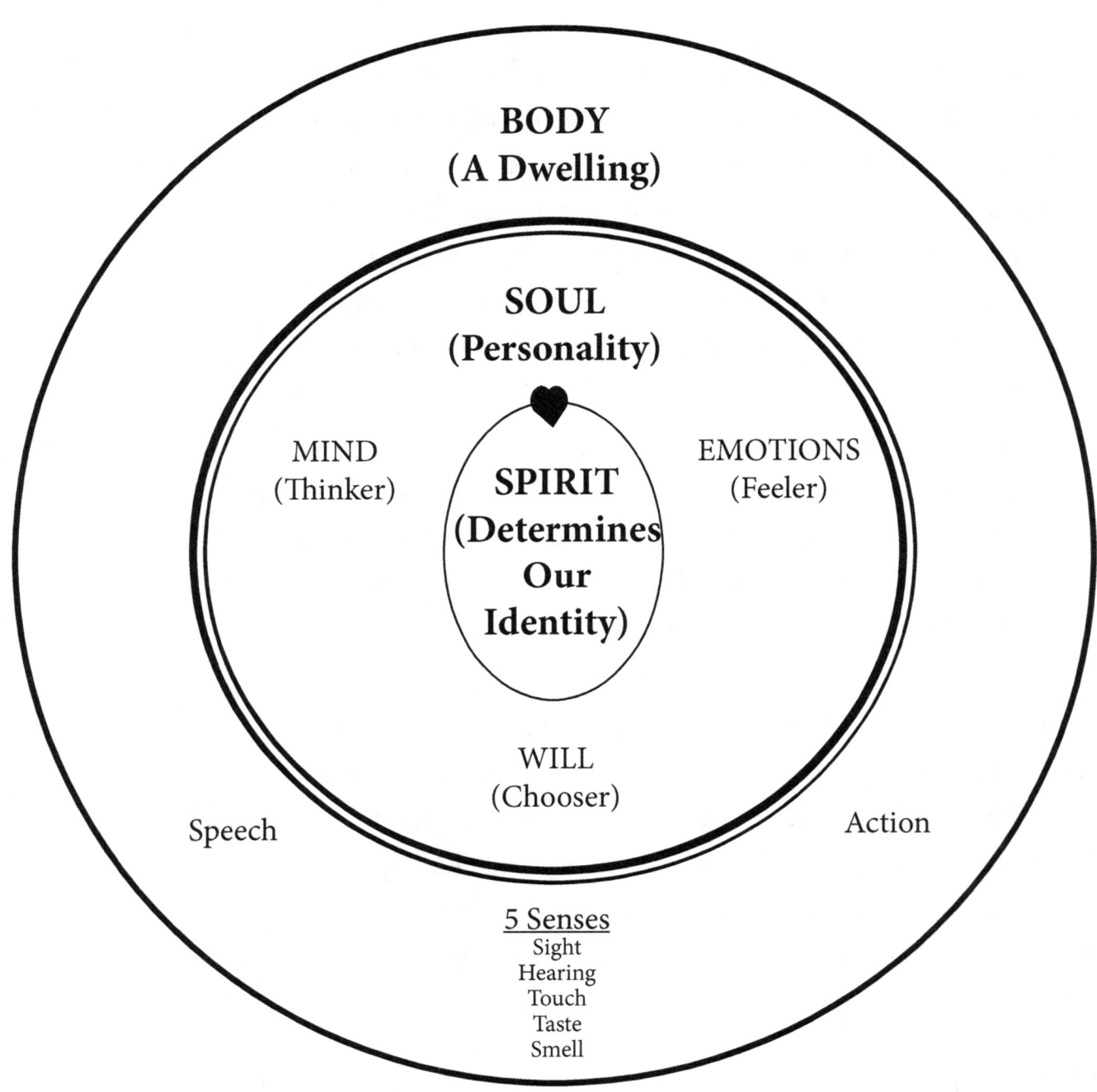

Brokenness is God's pruning process. Pain yields the most fruit in your life. Are you willing to let the deepest parts of God touch the deepest parts of you? Relationship with the Holy Spirit takes time.

–John Paul Jackson

The soul includes the mind, will, and emotions that together enable us to think, feel, and make decisions (Romans 12:2). We are to renew our minds and work out our salvation with fear and trembling.

The spirit has a three-fold purpose: communion, intuition, and conscience. We worship through communion, which is the spirit's ability to meet and experience another spirit. We can commune with the Holy Spirit or another spirit. But if we belong to God, our spirit is tuned in to the Holy Spirit. Another spirit can influence us through our minds if we have wrong motives, willful sin in our lives, or unforgiveness.

Intuition is to know or learn without conscious reasoning. Some gifts of the Holy Spirit flow out of intuition because the gifts seeminigly flow out of your spirit into your mind. *(This explains how people have ESP or psychic abilities, but the Holy Spirit is not the source.* Because it flows through the soul without being initiated by the Holy Spirit, it is an unholy spirit operating through them.) If you are a believer, the Holy Spirit is in you and wants to reach your world through you. That could be with teaching, preaching, healing, acts of kindness, giving, serving, discernment, words of knowledge, words of wisdom, and so forth. We hold back when we think it depends on our ability instead of on the Holy Spirit who lives in each of us as believers.

The conscience acknowledges moral rightness. It's the part of the spirit where God has written his Law, enabling us to know right from wrong. We have a choice about whether we obey it or the desires of the flesh, that is, the carnal nature that wants to control our minds. The Holy Spirit who dwells in us will convict us about what is right.

The body, which is to be redeemed, includes the five senses: sight, touch, taste, smell, and hearing. Dr. Henry Malone in his book, *Shadow Boxing*, explains victorious daily spiritual warfare as it regards the senses in this way:

> "Satan attacks our body with disease, the mind with lies and deception, and he laces our will with rebellion. Our delicate emotions are fragmented and hardened by pride, fear, jealousy, etc. This is why we should never allow our emotions to rule us. I might not feel like getting up early on Sunday morning, but my spirit is willing, makes the decision, my mind comes into agreement, and my body follows what my spirit dictates."

 **God Moment:**

Close your eyes and hear this…

My Child, don't be afraid to come to Me with all the things that bring you shame. I already know all about it, and as soon as you repented, I forgot about it. I am not the One bringing it up to you all the time.

Allow my Word to wash you and remove the stain and pain of your past. I was there, and I shed tears with you and wanted to comfort you then — so allow Me to comfort you now. There is nothing in your past that I can't redeem.

Draw near to Me, come under the shelter of my wings, and I will anoint you with the Holy Spirit and set you high on the Rock.

Psalm 27:5

Psalm 61:4

Assignment:

Ask the Lord to show you where your image of Him is too small. Ask Him what the bricks are that make up your wall.

_____
_____
_____

What were you brought up to believe about God?

_____
_____
_____

How has this lesson changed what you believe about Satan's influence in your life and God's role?

_____
_____
_____

Final thought:

God is sovereign, but we still wrestle against evil.

Journal:

Lesson 5 — Good Guys vs. Bad Guys (Angels, Demons, and Us)

To operate in the spiritual realm, we need to be able to recognize (or discern) the nature of the things we may be dealing with.

Angels were created by God (Colossians 1:16) and are assigned various ranks. The order of creation was sons of God, then angels, (who, by the way, did not have wings) then demons who were either before or after the fall of Satan, and finally man somewhere after angels and maybe before demons. The word for angels means "strong ones;" they are either good or evil.

Ancient gods were lesser gods who ruled the nations after the Tower of Babel when God disinherited the nations and put them under the rule of these lesser gods (Deuteronomy 32:8). They are not all myths; many are real. They became corrupt when they embraced the worship that should have gone to God. When God judged them, they lost their immortality (Psalm 82.6).

After disinheriting the nations, Israel (the people) became God's new earthly family, through Jacob (the man, later known as Israel.)

Jesus came to redeem all the nations. This is why we are commanded to evangelize the nations, so we can bring them back to God. Colossians 1:15 says He is the image of the invisible God and the firstborn over all creation. The title "firstborn" refers to his exalted role or position, not the timing of His birth (Psalm 89:27). The firstborn son in Jewish custom meant that he inherited the leadership of the family and received a double portion of what belonged to the father. Colossians 1:12 says we are qualified to be partakers of the inheritance of the saints; we are joint heirs with Christ.

Jesus rules over all things created, in the natural and

supernatural realm, and we are seated with Him in the heavenly realm (Ephesians 2:6). As believers, we are the executors of His estate. If Christ is the head and we are the body, then we are His hands and feet. Our hearts should reflect His heart. Love should be our motive for everything we do, every action and reaction. We should always examine our hearts before we minister (Ephesians 6:12). Does the enemy have any place in me? Jesus cut the line, but is there still a hook in me that the enemy can tug on to cause a reaction? If so, that reaction has a bad root and will therefore produce bad fruit.

We have talked about how Adam and Eve gave their delegated authority on the earth over to Satan when they chose to disobey God in the Garden. They gave away their "right to rule." The Gospel of John refers to Satan as the prince of this world. The word for prince is "*archon*", which was used to denote the highest official in a city or a region in the Greco-Roman world. So Jesus is telling us that the highest ruling power over the cosmos (world and nature) is the evil prince Satan; the world is under his power.

If someone has authority, they have the power to bless or curse. Webster's dictionary says they have legal or rightful power; a right to command or to act — dominion, jurisdiction. Authority has the power of sway or controlling influence over others. Because Adam and Eve, through their disobedience, chose not to follow God, their original legal right to rule the earth was handed over to Satan. He now has the legal position to govern the earth that was first given to man. Since man gave it away, another man, Jesus, the Word made flesh, had to legally get it back.

Through Jesus' death and resurrection, He has taken it back and delegated it to us as believers. Now we have authority over evil spirits in the spiritual realm. We do not have power over people though. Because we are joint heirs with Jesus, whatever belongs to Him belongs to us; however, to be effective, we have to know what is ours. 1 John 3:8 says Jesus destroyed the works of the devil. We don't have to wait until we get to heaven to experience the benefits of Jesus' resurrection (Hebrews 2:14-15). The enemy has been disarmed.

The apostle Paul talks about being a good soldier (2 Timothy 2:4), fighting the good fight (1 Timothy 1:18, 6:12), waging war (2 Corinthians 10:3), and struggling with a cosmic enemy (Ephesians 6:12).

The New Testament tells us to expect bad things as a part of life (John 16:33). Too often in the West, Christians attempt to intellectually understand evil, whereas New Testament Christians grappled with overcoming evil.

You'll notice that despite Christ's victory, the New Testament defines the Christian life in warfare terms. The outcome of the war is settled, but we still have battles to fight on a personal level. Fighting them is what the Christian life is all about. The confidence and hope of the believer is that Christ has once and forever defeated the enemy.

Discussion

As a Christian, do you expect God to protect you from struggling in life? Why or why not?

You might ask, *isn't God in control?* Yes, but remember the Garden? God doesn't micromanage our lives. He still gives us choices. Where good exists, evil will exist too. All that God created is good, but the natural laws we live under (such as gravity) dictate that evil will exist along with good. Look at the natural world: you cannot have light without darkness, cold without hot, or front without back. Having one automatically defines its opposite. God gave us a free will so we can choose to live in darkness or in the light. I don't believe things always go God's way, but I do know He will use everything for His glory and for our good because He is a loving God (Romans 8:28).

Christians live in this decaying world that is under Satan's rule. The early Church knew the reason there was evil in the world was because Satan is evil and everything about him is the opposite of good. I don't believe God brings on the evil that attacks Christians. We live in a universe where there is a principle of opposites. One thing in existence naturally brings its opposite along with it. Only by defining the law (righteousness) could people understand sin, or what it was to break the law of God.

In order to be able to choose righteousness, Adam and Eve had to be free to choose sin as well. Otherwise there is no choice, and God is a dictator. They chose to sin.

It is hard to reconcile that God is sovereign when we still wrestle against evil. We don't have all the answers as to why some people are subjected to such evil, especially children.

The early Church understood spiritual warfare; they expected opposition from the enemy. After all, he is the Adversary. They also knew Satan was a defeated foe.

Author and pastor Chip Ingram had this to say about Satan during his "*Diabolical*" series (broadcast 8/2/16):

> *A lion roars to create fear, to immobilize or isolate. When a lion wants to attack, it is stealthy. A lion won't attack until it is about 10-30 meters from its target. They stealthily move and attack that which is unaware; it can be healthy or sick, strong or weak, it doesn't matter. This is unlike other animals that only*

prey on the weak or sickly. Lions can be extremely fast for the 10-30 meters, but they have very little endurance. When we stand strong the enemy will eventually give up.

Satan wants to isolate you and create fear and self-condemnation, causing you to withdraw from people ... and withdraw from God's Word to isolate you no matter how strong a Christian you are. The attack will come when you are alone and vulnerable.

You can read what the Bible has to say about lion attacks in 1 Peter 5:8-9.

Discussion:

Can you think of a time when you knew you were missing the will of God because you made a decision that left you feeling "sick at heart," or with the feeling that you have done something wrong or missed something? How did the enemy use this to attack you?

Preparation for spiritual battles.

These teachings in Ephesians are important in preparing for spiritual battles.

> *Chapter 1: Our Identity in Christ.* We become programmed to think a certain way about ourselves, but God tells us our identity: we are holy (Ephesians 1:1), we are wrapped up in Christ (1:3), chosen (1:4), joined to Christ (1:7), claimed by God as his own inheritance (1:11), engaged as a bride (1:14), and we are His inheritance (1:18).
>
> *Chapter 2: Authority (Know the enemy is already defeated by the blood of Jesus.)* We are seated with Christ and given authority (Ephesians 2:6), and we have the

power of the Holy Spirit living in us (2:22).

Chapter 3: The Need for Fellowship and Community (The banana that leaves the bunch gets peeled.) Coming together with the Church as part of the Body of Christ (3:1-7) allows you to see the importance of being connected with other believers, so that we can be rooted and grounded in love (3:9).

Chapter 4: Walking in Unity with Each Other (Iron sharpens iron.) Unity is one's responsibility to pursue diligently (4:2-6) and can be found in the union of the Church (4:11-16).

Chapter 5: Walking in Love /Having Order in the Home. God demostrates love and gentleness toward us and encourages us to demonstrate gentleness and love toward one another (5:5).

Chapter 6: Instruction on Warfare. When facing sprirtual warfare, it is crucial to put on the armor of God before entering battle (6:11-18).

If any of the above are not in place in our lives, we can open the door for the enemy to have a "legal right" to oppress us.

In order to be effective in battle, we must know our identity in Christ, walk in our authority, have those we are in community with to hold us up and support us, be in unity with those around us, and be prepared and ready for battle.

Sometimes God will line up the circumstances in our lives to teach us things and cause us to look within so we can be healed and delivered. However, I believe Satan is the author of evil, not God (John 10:10-11).

So with that in mind, let's look at the good guys versus the bad guys.

From these names describing supernatural beings we know the following:

- *Elohim* is a plural term that many scholars believe clearly refers to lesser gods, i.e., sons of God, literally with "supernatural, great strength" (Hebrews 2:6-7; Psalms 8:1-8). There were many "elohim" but one true God over them who is Elohim Yahweh.

- Holy Ones "*Kadoshim*" literally means "separated ones" — holy ones who are devoted to God and are called holy ones (Psalm 89:6-7; Job 5:1, 15:15; Daniel 8:13).

- Stars denote heavenly nature and abode (Job 38:7); angels and stars are called the host of heaven (Deuteronomy 4:19, 17:3). Nehemiah 9:6 and Psalm 33:6 say the host of heaven worships the Lord; Jeremiah 19:13; Acts 7:39-43; 2 Kings 23:5, 10, 24, and Deuteronomy 18:10-14 all condemn astrology, demon worship, divination, and worship of stars, etc. Even though he knew the truth, Satan rebelled and caused other stars (angels) to also sin (Revelation 12:3-4). The stars were meant to reveal the gospel. However, Satan has completely perverted the true meaning of the signs of the Zodiac,[2] and reading your horoscope or planning your life based on what it says your future path should be is wrong and forbidden by God. Only God determines our future (Deuteronomy 4:19).

---

[2] *Primeval Astronomy: Gospel in the Stars*, by Joseph Seiss, 1882.

 **God Moment:**

Close your eyes and hear this ...

Beloved, even when you know you made a mistake and you cannot go back and change what happened, your repentance can change your future. Learn to recognize and follow the gentle leading of the Holy Spirit.

If you listen to that still small voice that comes from inside your spirit, you will have no regrets. Spend time in My Presence focusing on hearing My voice and being obedient to what you hear.

Don't be intimated; follow My gentle leading; trust Me.

1 Kings 19:11-12

John 10:27

Isaiah 30:15

Assignment:

Have you ever considered Satan's role in your circumstances? Explain.

_____
_____
_____

Describe how you can look back now and see things differently.

_____
_____
_____

When has God lined up the circumstances in your life to teach you things and cause to you to look within yourself so you could be healed and delivered?

_____
_____
_____

What did you learn from that experience?

_____
_____
_____

Final thought:

It is Satan who comes to steal, kill, and destroy; Jesus came to give us life more abundantly.

Journal:

Lesson 6 — Genuine Reality

The source of all great spiritual conflict is Satan.

You may hear of people praying for or to angels, or talk about having encounters with them. But are all these interactions and experiences from God? It was quite popular a few years ago for those in the New Age movement to worship angels. Satan uses this general interest and belief in angels to deceive us. As a result, it's important to know the real truth about God's heavenly beings, so you can recognize evil spirits when you encounter them and not be fooled.

Dr. J.P. Moreland, a Christian apologist, explained it to a group of his students at Talbot School of Theology this way:

"There are kooks out there — fair enough. All these things can be abused, including spiritual gifts. All I'm telling you is that there are credible people out there, who are not kooks, who are seeing things happen, and it's real."

Then he went on to detail a time in his life when he was preaching, and one of the members of the congregation came to him afterwards and told him that he saw three warrior angels standing behind him while he'd been preaching. The person told J.P. that when he saw them, he assumed that J.P. must be under tremendous attack, and began praying for him. It was very encouraging to Dr. Moreland, who passed on to his students the fact that, *"You are not alone. God sees you, loves you, and likes you."*

At a later time, he was struggling with anxiety, and he prayed about the angels, asking God if they were still there, and if not to please send them back, and if so (since he himself couldn't see them), for God to find a way to let him know. Within a week, he got a call from one of his friends, who was not prone to visions, telling him that recently during one of his lectures, for a period of about 5-10 minutes, he had seen three angels, one behind him, and one on each side of him. Because the vision was so unusual, the friend had been hesitant to mention it to Dr. Moreland, but finally felt impressed to do so.

Again, Dr. Moreland drew lessons from this for his students: *"Your heart was made for drama, we hunger for it … [and] the drama of the Kingdom of God against the kingdom of darkness is the greatest drama there is, and it's real. Now you can consider all of this an odd coincidence, but either way, cast your burdens on Him. He loves you."*

Angel in Greek is "*anglos*;" in Hebrew it's "*malak*." Its meaning is literally a messenger employed for purposes of God (Luke 1:11; Daniel 10:12, 18) or to execute His purposes (Psalms 104:4; Matthew 4:6; Psalms 91:11; Revelation 16:1; Hebrew 1:13-14).

They also execute God's judgments, such as plagues (Revelation 8:7-9:2), serve as watchers or supervisors and agents, and even control world government (Daniel 4:13, 17).

Michael the Archangel is the chief of the warring angels and guardian of Israel (Daniel 10:13, 21). Jewish tradition says Michael was one of seven Archangels. He was more concerned with the affairs of Israel and in the governmental structure of warring angels. That is why we see him warring against Satan where Israel is concerned. In Jude 9, he argued with Satan over the body of Moses. (Perhaps Satan thought he had a legal right to it because of Moses' disobedience in striking the rock the second time and because Moses had murdered an Egyptian.)

Gabriel had a different role. He was a messenger for God (Daniel 9:21; Luke 1:19, 26). Revelation 12:1-13 tells us that Satan was cast down to earth, not hell. The first heaven is the one we can see; his abode is the second heaven (a realm we cannot see). The third heaven is where God's throne is; it's beyond the second heaven (2 Corinthians 12:2). We see a glimpse of the second heaven in Daniel.

Satan has a chain of command and a ruling order that he governs, but God has placed Jesus over everything.

Satan has a counterfeit on earth (first heaven) for everything in the (third) heavenly realm.

Here are some examples:
- Christ: Anti-Christ, False Apostles, Prophets, and Teachers
- Miracles: Magic, Healings, Tongues, Revelation, Doctrine
- Freedom: Bondage
- Developing a person's full potential: suppressing potential and creativity, destruction
- Communion: we drink wine, Satanists drink blood
- Baptisms: we are baptised to symbolize death to our old lives, and rebirth to a new one as we are empowered by the Holy Spirit to live for Christ. Satanists are baptised to receive a new demon spirit to empower them to live for Satan.

The point is that Satan cannot create, so he has to copy and reverse what is real. For this reason, you have to be careful not to be led away by a partial truth.

I'm told that when Secret Service agents want to learn to recognize counterfeit money, they train by studying the real thing. By knowing the real thing in intricate detail, they easily know the counterfeit when they see it. When you are well-acquainted with the Holy Spirit on a personal level, you will also recognize what is counterfeit.

💗 Instead of getting hung up on the counterfeit, ask the Lord to show you the real thing.

Hierarchies in both worlds.

Just as there is a hierarchy of the angelic realm, there is a hierarchy of the demonic realm. They both have thrones in the spirit realm, and they will set up thrones in a person's soul. That will be where the strong man (See Mark 3:27) is encamped. He will try to dominate your thinking, feelings, and actions from there.

Feelings can be triggered even when there is no memory. We now believe that memories start at two months of gestation when there are no words to express the feelings. Your brain starts recording when things don't go well, e.g., parents fighting, feelings of rejection, etc. Children who have been given up for adoption especially struggle with rejection even though loving parents have adopted them.

My niece committed suicide because she could not get past her perceived rejection of being given up for adoption. Before her death, she could have contacted her biological father but was too afraid of more rejection, so she never did. That wasn't the only contributing factor, but it certainly played a part in her tragic choices.

Discussion:

How would a strongman in an area of our soul affect us?

Cherubim are those we call angels, but in the heavenly hierarchy they seem to rank above angels; perhaps they are divine beings called the sons of God. They are beings that cover the Mercy Seat and who worship God (Genesis 3:24; Ezra 1; Revelation 4:6-9). Seraphim (Isaiah 6:1-8) are thought to be burning, fiery, gliding, angelic beings. They may be angels of a fiery color or appearance, or flame-like in motion or clearness. We see the four faces of the Cherubim in the four gospels. Scholars frequently use the symbolism of Man, Lion, Ox, and Eagle to represent the four Gospels of Matthew, Mark, Luke and John, respectively; the same four beings are depicted as the heads of Cherubim in Ezekiel 1:6. (Cherubim are not angels.)

The following picture is artist Drew Pryor's depiction of what Cherubim may look like:

In addition to being messengers, angels are ministers of God.

- They reveal God's will, purposes and Word (Acts 7:53; Matthew 1:20-25; Daniel 9:20; Revelation 1:1, 22:6,8).

- They protect God's people (Genesis 32:1-32; Daniel 6:20-23; Hebrews 1:14; 2 Kings 6:16).

- They deliver God's people, (Revelation 7:1-14; Acts 5:17-20, 12:5-10) including Peter from prison.

- They strengthen and encourage God's people (Matthew 4:11; Luke 22:43; Acts 5:19-20, 27:23-25); in 1 Kings 19 angels ministered to Elijah.

You'll find them throughout the Bible protecting and delivering God's people. They also strengthen and encourage us when we are in need. In each instance, you see that angels are messengers for God.

Hebrews 1:7 says they were created to serve God and are sent by Him to help us. However, they are subject to His command, not ours. They are also not baby-ish creatures floating on clouds, but massive, powerful, awe-inspiring beings. Gabriel was the chief messenger angel; when we see him, he usually begins with, "fear not," because with his commanding presence, fear is the first natural reaction.

Keeping our priorities straight

It is important to renew our minds with the Word of God and not let our thinking or feelings dictate our decisions. Our spirit is safe from the enemy, but our mind, body, and emotions are not yet redeemed. This is why we need to be aware of Satan's strategies.

In 2 Corinthians 3:17-18 Paul begins with the spirit because that is where God first nourishes and strengthens us for warfare. Next, our soul is nourished. Then, the body will begin to experience a change because it will follow the dictates of the spirit when the mind agrees with the truth of what God says. "Transformed into His image" means that as the Word brings life, we are changed.

Every action begins with a thought, and whatever dominates your thinking will dominate your actions.

Wrong Thinking

The owner of a tattoo parlor was asked why so many people came in to get tattoos that reflect darkness (such as skeletons, skull and cross bones, etc.). He said, "Because before there is ever a tattoo on the body, there is a tattoo on the mind." It was a profound insight, because we will manifest in our body whatever is already in our mind, whether it is good or bad.

Keep in mind that a tattoo is hard to get rid of. Removing it is a painful process, and most of the time you can still see it, or at least the scar is visible. You can't remove the tattoo on your own; you need help in having it removed. The same is true for wrong thinking. It involves renewing your mind with the Word of God and the Holy Spirit, allowing truth to penetrate and bring God's perspective to your situation. Sometimes that can be a painful process.

We know Paul suffered from a thorn in the flesh; however, we don't know if that was emotional turmoil or a physical condition. I'm sure he struggled with the fact that he persecuted and murdered his fellow Israelites who were believers, causing him guilt and condemnation. His defense, as well as ours, is that it is all under the blood of Jesus and covered by grace when we confess, repent, and forgive (1 Thessalonians 5:23).

We can counter Satan's attacks when we know the difference between conviction and condemnation:

- Recognize his strategy and make a different choice, asking the Holy Spirit to guide us.
- Realize that tormenting thoughts do not come from God.
- Repent of pride, thinking we can do it ourselves without God.
- Recognize the difference between *conviction* (always has hope) and *condemnation* (which offers no hope).
- Remember or find and apply appropriate scripture to your situation.
- Rely on grace.
- Realize that after we confess and repent of our past sins, they are under the blood of Jesus.

Discussion:

How is Satan targeting you?

Good vs. Evil:

Angels always worship and rejoice in the works of God, always execute God's will, have influence over the affairs of nations, watch over the interest of Churches, assist and protect believers, are used to punish God's enemies, perform extraordinary acts on behalf of God's people, and minister personally to each of God's children.

Demons always worship and serve Satan in fear, always execute his will, are committed to attacking humans, and where possible, keeping them from being saved; they radically oppose committed Christians and are strategically involved in the affairs of nations through territorial ruling princes.

They oppose the interests of Churches, oppose and attack believers, and will do all they can to attack God's children through sickness, accidents, finances, and relationships. They also perform extraordinary acts on behalf of Satan (Think about the Egyptian magicians who copied many of Moses' plagues originally ordained by God to prove Moses spoke for Him); in short, demons will try to make humans turn away from knowing the one true God. But for all of that, remember:

Demons are subject to our command because, as believers, we have been delegated the authority of Jesus.

You were saved for a purpose

In Ephesians, Paul emphasizes that we have been saved not only for our personal benefit, but also to bring praise and glory to God. The climax of God's purpose, "when the times have reached their fulfillment," is to bring all things in the universe together under Christ (Ephesians 1:10). It is crucially important for Christians to understand this, so in Ephesians 1:15-23 Paul prays for their understanding.

-from The Glo Bible introduction to Ephesians.

Having explained God's great goals for the Church, Paul proceeds to show the steps toward their fulfillment. First, God has reconciled individuals to himself as an act of grace (Ephesians 2:1-10). Second, God has reconciled these saved individuals to each other. Then, He united us as one body, the Church. Paul states that what God has intended for the Church is that it be the means by which He displays His "manifold wisdom" to the "rulers and authorities in the heavenly realms" (Ephesians 3:7-13). He makes it clear by the repeated use of the term "heavenly realms" that Christian existence is not merely on an earthly plane. It receives its meaning and significance from heaven, where Christ is exalted at the right hand of God (Ephesians 1:20). He will use the Church to bring the nations back to Himself.

Discussion:

We are to have an impact in the heavenly realm. What would that look like in your life?

Ephesians 6:10-20 indicates that we are to be armed and equipped as soldiers. And certainly the Church is an elite group of soldiers, but we need training. We have been empowered to live victoriously and to evangelize the nations by bringing them back to God, but we must also remember that only the Holy Spirit can work from the inside out in order to change hearts.

Only the Holy Spirit in us can defeat the enemy and bring victory based on the blood of Jesus.

What We Don't See is as Real as What We Do See

As we mentioned earlier, Satan was cast out of heaven. **Revelation 12:1-12** seems to be a picture of Israel giving birth to the Messiah. I believe Satan was cast out of heaven *after* the resurrection of Christ **(verse 10)**; therefore, he can no longer come into heaven and accuse us before God as he did Job. **Hebrews 9:12, 21-26** says that Jesus took His blood into heaven and cleansed the heavens.

Ephesians 4:8-10 tells of how Jesus led a host of captives and gave gifts to men, but first He descended into the lower parts of the earth. Many interpret this to mean that He released the righteous dead from that place and took them with Him to heaven. I think they were "in holding" in a place called Paradise because heaven had to be cleansed before they could live there.

Discussion:

What are some ways Satan began to corrupt mankind?

We said in a previous lesson that **Isaiah 14:4-15** portrays Satan as King of Babylon; **Ezekiel 28:12-17** makes it pretty clear that Satan is also the spirit behind the King of Tyre. He used these kings to manifest his corrupt ways. In **Revelation 12:9** there was war in heaven and he was thrown out. We know from elsewhere in scripture that after the rebellion he was no longer called *Lucifer (light)*, but *Satan – adversary or one who opposed God*. Satan became a fiend who epitomizes all that is unholy and evil.

As Lucifer, he was probably over worship in heaven. This is an interesting thought because he will do whatever it takes to keep us from ascending in worship to exalt the Lord. He knows that worship creates an atmosphere in which he can't exist.

Now Satan wants man to serve and worship him; he also wants to undo God's work (Mark 4:15). Job 2:4-5 shows us that he wants to cause man to renounce God.

Watch very carefully the ways in which Satan will try to confuse. His oldest strategy is to take what is actually said and confuse the listener by convincing them they heard something different. This is much like the old children's game of gossip, where the first child whispers something to the second, who repeats it in a whisper to the third child, and so on down the line. The last child always gets an entirely different message than the one that was originally started.

It is hard to look at the spiritual realm and believe it is as real as the world we see and touch, but it is (2 Corinthians 4:18).

Discussion:

Have you ever been shocked to find out something was going on right under your nose or right next door, and you had no idea at the time? Maybe something so crazy that you wouldn't have believed it until it all came out in the open and you found out it was true?

The book *Room*

In the book *Room*, which is now a movie, a man kidnaps a woman, and holds her captive in an enclosed space. She becomes pregnant and has a little boy. They are actually living in a shed in the man's backyard. Her son, Jack, believes the room they are confined in is the whole world because that's all he has ever known during his five years on earth. He has never been exposed to anything outside that room except through a skylight in the roof where he a can see a patch of sky and the occasional contrail from an airplane. They have a television with poor reception, but he thinks the people on the set are not real. After escaping, he discovers the real world.

The story is fictional, but the message is real: Just because something is outside our realm of seeing, hearing, touching, and believing doesn't keep it from being true. If we have never experienced it, seen it, or felt it, that doesn't make it nonexistent. Sometimes we have to get outside of our box of experience to realize something is real that we had a misconception about.

The spirit realm is as real as the physical, and the fact that we can't see it, feel it, or touch it doesn't negate that fact. We may not believe it, but it is still true. Our personal experience doesn't always dictate reality one way or the other. Demons are involved in the events of life so we need to consider the role they play when we seek to explain and deal with the events of our lives.

Since the human spirit is the only one assigned to a physical body who lives in the physical realm, demon spirits will fight to gain dominion of that body (Luke 11:24-26).

Satan is a real person (John 8:41-44).

The Lake of Fire is for Satan and his angels (Matthew 25:41; Revelation 20:7-15). Those who shared in his rebellion will share in his judgment, but we have been redeemed from sharing in the curse on man (Galatians 3:13-14) because Jesus became a curse for us. That's another reason why fallen angels and the demonic realm hate mankind so much. We can be redeemed and our sins forgiven, while for them there is no hope of redemption.

Demons are referred to as evil angels in Revelation 12:9 and 2 Peter 2:4. They were given bounds, and some went beyond those boundaries in Genesis 6:2. Jude 6-8 says they went after strange flesh. 2 Peter 2:4-5 says they did not keep their assigned boundaries. These are the angels; the ones who after leaving their first estate went after strange flesh, the ones that are kept in chains. Angels who were on assignment from God have special permission to take on human form, but those who are mentioned here did it without permission. We see in Job 1:12 and Matthew 8:29 that God had placed both boundaries and time limits on Satan and evil spirits. They were not allowed to go beyond those boundaries without divine permission. If this interpretation of scripture is correct, corrupt spiritual beings went outside the boundaries of God when they came down to marry women, and produced the giants who were evil (Genesis 6:1-4). Perhaps this is why God said that he regretted he had made man (Genesis 6:6).

Jesus related to man through the virgin birth; the Holy Spirit was involved, but no angel was involved. Through His death and resurrection, mankind was redeemed.

 **God Moment**

Close your eyes and listen…

Child, don't ever doubt that you are Mine. I bought you with a great price. Don't let My blood be shed in vain; appropriate all I've done for you. Ask Me for whatever you need then listen for My response.

Keep your eyes on Me and guard your heart from doubting. Ask Me to search your heart for any unforgiveness. If My light reveals it, repent and forgive as I've forgiven you.

Pray for those who have wounded you and despitefully used you.

1 Corinthians 6:20

Isaiah 53:4-5

Matthew 5:44 (KJV)

Assignment:

In what way has Satan tried to bring corruption to your family?

_____
_____
_____
_____

When and how has God moved you out of your comfort zone and had you step outside the box?

_____
_____
_____
_____

Final thought:

Jesus came to set us free from Satan's corruption of man.

Lesson 7 — Demonization, Possession, and Oppression

Genesis 1:28 quotes God as telling Adam, "Be fruitful and multiply and fill the earth and subdue it, and have dominion … over every living thing that moves on the earth." So mankind was never intended to *stay* in the Garden of Eden. It was to be a home base, a place from which to launch into the rest of the world.

Just to review, as humans, we were to be God's hands on earth. It was a big mission. Like any good parent, God gave us His very best, and wanted the best for us. But He also wanted a genuine relationship with us, so He gave us the gift of choice. He wanted us to freely choose to follow Him, and without free will, the relationship He wanted would be impossible. So along with the directive to be fruitful and multiply throughout the earth, in Genesis 2:15-17, He told Adam not to eat of the Tree of the Knowledge of Good and Evil in the Garden. In Genesis 3, Adam and Eve chose death rather than life. They ate of the forbidden tree.

After the Fall, the life man had enjoyed in the Garden ceased to exist. Even today the enemy keeps influencing mankind, even some of God's own children. This is where it can get controversial, and many sincere Christians tend to believe Christ-followers are immune to demonic influence. However, I can tell you from personal experience, that is only partially true. Let me explain.

There is a difference between possession and oppression.

Possession vs. oppression

The transliteration of the Greek term *diamonizo* is "demonized" and sometimes rendered "demoniacs" (*Jewish New Testament*

Commentary, David Stern). The term "possessed" might be too strong and inflexible to use for the level of demonic activity usually encountered in Christian people (Mark 5:18; Luke 9:42).

Paul in Ephesians 4:27 says not to give the devil a foothold (an opportunity), *topas,* which is literally "a place." Some of the strongest opportunities or footholds a person can offer the enemy are: anger, self-hatred, bitterness, and unforgiveness. The imagery here is of an enemy who is not strong enough to conquer (or possess) a country (that is, a Christian) but can establish a small beachhead from which he can carry out raids and cause turmoil. An example of this would be when one takes on an offense and won't forgive. Unforgiveness gives the enemy a place from which to influence every area of their life. Everything is then filtered through that lens or beachhead.

This can start small, or be as extreme as when Satanic cults prey on Christians or communities where Christians exercise no power. (Fortunately, where Christians are strong and praying, the Satanists have no influence over that area.) But whether it's unforgiveness or Satanic influence, the principle is the same: don't give a place to evil in your life.

Discussion:

Does the enemy have a beachhead or stronghold in your life? Where does he operate from in order to dominate your thoughts or behavior to steal, kill, and destroy?

The Holy Spirit in a believer can set up a spiritual control center, which no demon can overcome. But this is not necessarily automatic. It requires being willing to be led by the Spirit, and to listen to God. Your choices are an important part of the control center because you must be obedient to what you hear. Prayer and obedience are required as well as repentance and forgiveness.

Demonic activity seems to be limited to the mind and body of a believer. Satan cannot overthrow the reign of Christ in a believer. Although our spirits are sealed with the Holy Spirit, our minds have to be renewed. Satan will use a little truth in what he says and does, just enough to cause us to fall into deception. This is why it's critical that we know the Word, stay close to God, and listen as He reveals truth to us. Taking our thoughts captive, too, is extremely important in warfare, as outlined in 2 Corinthians 10:3-5. When we let our emotions rule, we get into trouble far more easily.

The fiery darts of the evil one will get through if we don't use our spiritual resources, and as a result, he will gain ground in our lives. Prayer, praise, and scripture (the offensive Sword of the Spirit, Ephesians 6:17) are our greatest defensive weapons when this happens. However, it isn't easy when we are in the midst of the battle. This is why we are to put on our spiritual armor mindset every day (Ephesians 6:11-13) so that we are always ready.

To recover and reinforce your freedom:

- Break ties with the spirit realm where Satan rules, by repenting, confessing, and forgiving yourself and others, sometimes even God.

- See yourself seated with Christ in the throne room.

- Begin to rule and reign with Christ as you live above your circumstances instead of always under them (Ephesians 2:6).

- Remember you have a new identity; you are no longer a victim, but instead you are more than a conqueror (Romans 8:37).

- Develop a thankful heart.

Demonization can start from within or without.

From Outside: Believers and non-believers alike can experience temptations, oppression, and hassles that affect the function of a person, and result in obsession. Satan first tries to take control of the mind; then the body will follow the dictates of the mind/soul. Many attacks that start from the outside move to the inside when we come into agreement with them and act upon them. We are particularly vulnerable to this in the instance of fear-based issues.

From Inside: (demonization happens through the soul — not the spirit —of a believer.) Evil spirits hold and gain ground in a person's life, which becomes inhabitation. I believe the enemy can hold ground in a Christian's life without possessing them. Evil spirits can dominate an area because of trauma, unforgiveness (such as in relationships) or through generational trauma or sin. For example, I had a phobia — the fear of frogs — that was passed down to me from my mother. Sometimes a stronghold is through wrong beliefs. Examples: 1) we might think that *if my mother had this, I will too,* 2) it's true because *my church says it is,* 3) a wrong diagnosis *because my doctor said so.* Demonization can take various forms, from persecution and harassment, to being captivated by false teaching, and to enslavement to sin. It can include obsessive-compulsive disorder, hypochondria, phobias, and so on. Paul's thorn in the flesh, for example, was a demonic being — he called it a "messenger of Satan" (2 Corinthians 12:7).

For Non-Christians: For non-Christians, when demons have complete control, it becomes what we've called possession. When an unbeliever has episodes of what we call "possession," they are being controlled by demons. However, they still have free will when a demon isn't in control, so I prefer the word "demonized" instead of "possession."

Degrees of Demonization

"Outside"		"Inside"	
Temptation Hassle	Hassle that affects function of person	"Hold or "ground" in a person's life	Demons have control
Oppression	**Obsession**	**Inhabitation**	**Possession**
Christians involved at these levels			Non-Christians

Stages of demonization:

There are seven stages of demonic influence in believers:

First, *Regression* – you start going back to old habits, old ways of thinking and living.

Next, *Repression* – you push down, bury, deny, or reject painful or disagreeable memories, impulses using shear willpower alone.

Third, *Suppression* – this is your conscious inhibition of impulses you may be feeling.

Fourth, *Depression* – prolonged and excessive sadness, lethargy.

Fifth, *Oppression* – a sense of heaviness you can't shake off.

Next, *Obsession* – something or someone that dominates your focus and your thinking.

And finally, *Possession* – demonized or demonization — dominates your actions.

There are (at least) eight signs that could indicate the presence of demonic influence:

1. Voices coming from inside your head that are not your own.
2. Obsessions and compulsions you cannot control (fears, perversions, addictions).
3. Constant feelings of guilt, condemnation, shame, rejection.

4. PTSD (Post Traumatic Stress Disorder).
5. A sense of being tormented.
6. Mental health disorders.
7. Anxiety.
8. Bi-polar disorder.

If we belong to God, then He "owns" us, and a demon can't own us as well, which is what the word *possession* indicates. Jesus drove the moneychangers out of the temple in the outer court (John 2:15). They were not in the Holy of Holies, which I believe is a picture of the Holy Spirit in our spirit. Likewise, a demon can't control our innermost part — our spirit — but can influence our "outer court" of body and mind.

Healing and Deliverance

While a demon can't own or possess us as believers, we sometimes do need others to pray for us in order to be free ourselves. We also need each other to hold onto our newfound freedom. This is why we are to live in community with other believers. We need to be willing to help other people find freedom and hold onto it because no one person has all the answers.

Remember that Truth is the antidote to Satan's deception. Deliverance comes with receiving truth – realizing we are more than conquerors (Romans 8:37). Again, we need others to help receive and maintain our own freedom, especially if we've made a pact with the devil, either willingly or unwillingly.

If you've been traumatized, you will usually need help to get healing.

Freedom through deliverance or healing prayer requires being transparent, admitting there is a problem, and being willing to receive help. Ask the Lord whom to trust.

In most cases, there is a sin root, so confession, renunciation, and repentance are keys to freedom, especially if there was a demonic pact with the devil, even if forced to do it.

Repentance means you are sorry, and it supernaturally reclaims the ground the enemy has stolen, currently or in the past. Renouncing something means you don't intend to do it again in the future. The problem may be unforgiveness or sin that goes back in your ancestral line (parents or grandparents), causing the need to repent on their behalf.

When trauma was involved, first there is usually a need for emotional healing, after which deliverance is usually easy.

Support for your deliverance requires an understanding of spiritual authority in the Church and exercising that authority over the demonic realm. After deliverance, there needs to be a church-based support group and a place of accountability with encouragement. Small groups or one-on-one ministry are best. Usually the person healed will need to learn to make different choices and respond differently (Romans 5:17; 21).

It's important to remember that A) you have been delegated spiritual authority and that B) it's not authority over people, but over the work of the enemy in the lives of people.

God Moment:

Close your eyes and listen . . .

Beloved, I hold you in the center of my hand and will never let you go. You are the apple of my eye and I delight in you. Don't let all I've done for you be in vain. Take advantage of all the benefits of the cross.

My son died so you could live, and live victoriously. Learn to walk in that victory. Don't be afraid to ask for help because I've placed you in a place where help is available; just humble yourself and ask. Take a risk; it will be worth it.

1 Samuel 18:22

1 Peter 2:24

Matthew 12:20

Assignment:

What are some things you struggle with on a daily basis?

_____
_____
_____
_____

What are some things you do to manipulate God so you can get what you want?

_____
_____
_____
_____

What are some things in your life are you not willing to give up?

_____
_____
_____
_____

Final Thought

Remember to do a daily heart check to make sure there are no open doors to the enemy

Journal:

Lesson 8: Understanding the Power of Evil Spirits

Satan wanted to corrupt the human race by polluting it.

Satan has assumed that if he can pollute mankind, then God won't be able to use the human race to defeat him. So control has became the issue. Satan wants to keep control of planet earth. God said He would not destroy the earth with another flood, so Satan tries to ruin the human race, and has been doing so since the flood (and perhaps before as well) (2 Corinthians 11:14-15). He always tests the Word of God (i.e., successfully with Eve in the Garden and unsuccessfully with Jesus in the wilderness. Jesus resisted him by using His spiritual Sword: the Word of God.)

Jesus is the Word. Applying the Word of God to your situation will always make a difference.

After God confused the languages, he disinherited the nations and assigned them to lesser gods who became corrupt. They caused mankind to worship themselves (in the form of idols) rather than the one true God.[3]

A part of Satan's pollution strategy included creating the gods of mythology. Whether these "gods" were a hybrid race, fallen angels, or figments of imagination, Satan used them to divert the culture to idol worship. Every ancient culture has stories about "star people" or gods coming down to earth and producing offspring. In Greek mythology the Titans were partly celestial and partly terrestrial. Legend has it they rebelled against their father Uranus, and after a prolonged contest, were defeated by Zeus and

---
3 See *The Unseen Realm*, by Michael Heiser.

condemned into Tartarus. Hermes was the Greek god of speed; the Roman version was Mercury. But it was the same demons controlling the different regions. We tend to believe mythology is a part of fiction, but perhaps those gods of mythology were real supernatural entities that had power to influence those regions. It's interesting that there are currently a lot of movies out about the gods of mythology, calling them superheroes.

By disguising themselves as either good, or at least harmless, demons work through unsuspecting humans to accomplish their purposes. They really try to gain a foothold with people in the church. I think Satan puts the same demonic spirits in each church to accomplish his purposes. He wants to render Christians to be spiritually ineffective.

Discussion:

Have you ever changed jobs or churches or moved to a new neighborhood and found that the same problems were going on there as the last place (i.e., the same toxic spirits were operating, like control, criticism, jealousy, etc., even though the faces were new, with different names)? Describe what you encountered.

For Noah to have been spared from God's judgment, he must have been untainted, separating himself from others of his day.

Sometime after the flood, his descendants began to practice pagan ways. At Babel, when He disinherited the nations, the Lord also confused their language and then scattered them as a judgment on human pride and self-rule. The name Babel is derived from the Hebrew *bale*, which means "mixed up" or "confused." Later the Babylonians interpreted "Babel" to mean "the gate of God." You can read the whole story of Babel in Genesis 10-11.

Hebrew and Christian tradition says that Nimrod, Noah's great-grandson, built a tower there called *Babel,* "the gate to heaven."

Babylon was founded by Nimrod, and was more than a city; it was Satan's control center over Mankind. In concert with Satan, Nimrod became the first leader of the post-flood world. Satan is a *religious* and *political* personality, and he used Nimrod for his purposes. He wants control of the world's political, religious, and economic structures.

Nimrod means "we will rebel," and his rebellion was against God. Satan found a prideful and willing human to come into agreement with his lies and to rebel against God. The ancient Christian writer Josephus said Nimrod wanted revenge on God. He built a tower, a pagan temple, too high to be flooded in case God wanted to bring another flood.

Ham, Cush, and Nimrod could be called the original unholy trinity. Many believed that like the pharoahs of Egypt, Cush, Nimrod, and his wife Semiramis were all three worshiped as gods. (Eusebius, a well-respected ancient biblical scholar and historian, identifies Semiramis as Nimrod's wife. She is not actually mentioned by name in the Bible.) We see in these three — Nimrod, Semi, and the child — an unholy trinity, which appears again in Revelation 12 and 13 with Satan, the Antichrist, and the False Prophet.

Nimrod and legends of idolatry

Nimrod first established his kingdom by founding a city on the plain in Shinar, that would later be called Babel, or Babylon. He is thought to be the originator of sun worship as well as founder of Babylon, located in Mesopotamia. It was the first world empire where he was king. He was known in Egypt as Osiris, as his wife claimed he would lift the curse placed on man and the earth. She was also known by the names Ishtar and Isis.

Some ancients say that after Nimrod died, Semiramis claimed she was his mother. This was so she could fulfill the prophecy in the Garden by claiming Immaculate Conception as his holy mother. Pictures of the two of them look amazingly like pictures of Jesus and the Virgin Mary. From this writing we see that, "after his death she claimed she had been visited by the spirit of Nimrod and had a child, Horus, that she said was the reincarnation of her deified husband, Nimrod," according to *Epic of Gilgamesh*

> "She was supposed to have ascended into heaven as the mother of the sun god and became the queen of heaven."
>
> —*Truth Matters*, Professor Walter J. Veith

The tower Nimrod designed was built with brick and mortar and was waterproof so if a flood came, it would still stand. He was actually building an altar. The belief is that he wanted mankind to look to him to meet their needs instead of God, so he set himself up as a god to be worshipped by men. Mankind was told in Genesis to spread out and replenish the earth, but Nimrod wanted to keep them close within his control.

It's also believed that Nimrod corrupted the meaning of the zodiac. The constellations originally had meanings that pointed to Jesus[4]. It is also believed that the Tower he built was an astrological temple with seven levels. According to *History World*, the Babylonians were the first great astrologers and introduced the zodiac.

Nimrod was also the first to organize men for war, and as we stated earlier, it is believed that he and his wife were the original gods. Supposedly, the name for her in Egypt was the goddess *Isis* (heavenly mother, magic) and for him *Horus* (god of the underworld).

---

4 *Primeval Astronomy: Gospel in the Stars*, Joseph Seiss, 1882.

The ancient deities are thought to have originated at Babylon because the origin of pagan religion and idolatry can be traced back to Cush and his son Nimrod along with his wife Semiramis.

The principalities of the lesser gods became known by the names of gods and goddesses worshipped by those nations (Deuteronomy 32:8; Psalms 82:6).

Gods and goddesses were the same in each culture but worshipped by different names. Nimrod's name was Mercury in Rome, and his wife's name was Minerva; in Greece his name was Hermes and his wife's name was Athena.

So it's believed that the Roman cult of Minerva was the same as that of Athena in the Grecian culture. Minerva (goddess of wisdom and war) is one the Olympians thought to have been born out of the head of Zeus, who was supposedly king of the gods and god of the sky and weather. He was the most powerful of all the ancient Greek and Roman gods and was supposedly worshipped as ruler of heaven and earth. He was also said to be a prince over all other gods and men. Minerva was worshipped as the goddess of wisdom, commerce, the arts, professions, schools, medicine, and war. She was the protector over cities. Her symbol is the owl.

Gods and goddesses were ruling spirits over countries and regions (the prince of Persia and the prince of Greece are examples in Daniel 10). Minerva was worshiped through magic, divination, incantations, sacrifices, prayers, and ritualistic dances. She was brash, arrogant, and strong-willed. Her name comes from the root *manus* or *mens*. She was dressed like a man and had decidedly masculine characteristics. Her reputation in war rivaled that of Mars, god of war.

The importance of names

Names of demons reflect their purpose or how they manifest through a person. For example, the root of the eating disorder anorexia is the goddess Ana. There is actually a cult that worships her through starving their bodies, and followers compete with each other to see who can stay the thinnest.

God even changed names in the Bible for spiritual significance. Your name reflects who you are and your character. For example, the great seal of California, the stamp of state authority and approval, is Minerva. On it, she is disguised as a mythological Roman goddess overlooking San Francisco Bay. I believe she is really a demonic prince over that region leading to the stronghold of sexual perversion.

Titan was the god of time, and Saturn was the Roman god of fertility and agriculture (these are names of demonic principalities that controlled the different empires of the world).

Scholars have connected Marduk, the Chief of Babylon (in Hebrew he's called Merodach), with Nimrod. In Aramaic he was called Bel (Lord). Female goddesses dominated the religious scene, i.e., Diana, Athena, and India's Kali, etc. The different names of gods and goddesses in different cultures were all the original god and goddess — thought to be Nimrod and Semiramis. They were names of the one "archetype" the names were merely variations.

In Freemasonry, the name of their god is Jabbulon and is an amalgam of the names of three gods, the middle of which represents Baal.

Revelation 17 speaks of the "mystery of Babylon the Great Mother of harlots and the abominations of the earth." In verse 15 it speaks of her influence over nations, peoples, and tongues. Could this be referring to Semiramis, the mother of idolatry in Babylon? The different cultures gave them different characteristics, but they were the same demon spirits.

It's interesting that when Paul cast a demon out of the girl in Acts 16:16-18, the spirit is called "a spirit of Apollo or Python." The girl had been possessed by a demon camouflaging itself as some famous mythological hero.

People who are being strongly influenced by the demonic need Christians to pray for them and point them to Christ. Both non-Christians and Christians alike need the church for support and accountability.

Demons are evil spirits with a will, intelligence, emotions (James 2:19 says they believe and tremble), and purpose; each has individual distinctive characteristics, which reflect their purpose (some mimic personalities). Plato derived the etymology of the word demon (*daimon* in Greek) for an adjective meaning "intelligent" or "knowing." This was the spirit that would come to men giving advice, often wise advice, suggesting that intelligence is a prominent characteristic of speech by demons. So they can communicate with us, but it is corrupted by their pride and arrogance.

- They speak (Luke 4:33-35; Luke 4:41).
- They choose to live somewhere. (Matthew 12:43-45).
- They are powerful (Acts 19:16-17).
- They have limited knowledge (Acts 19:15).
- Their goal is to ruin man morally, physically, and mentally for eternity.
- They want to control a person's mind and body.

- They want your will to come into agreement with theirs.
- They wait for open doors like sin, trauma, childhood circumstances (Satan does not play fair), or inheritance.

Unforgiveness is a huge open door for the enemy. In Matthew 18:21-35 it caused the man to be turned over to the tormentors: demonic spirits.

Demons don't usually announce their presence.

Even a Christian can allow demons to dominate and hold ground in certain areas of his/her life (i.e., food, hoarding, spending, lying, unforgiveness, pornography, or anger).

Be forewarned that when you are praying for someone to be set free in some area, a demon might manifest. The person may have a feeling that something is dominating them. Or if they can't overcome the problem no matter what they do and know, then they need help to be free. Severe trauma will usually have a demon attached to it. A person who is disassociated and in an altered state will have a demon attached.

Don't be afraid of this, but stand firm and rebuke it. When you rebuke it, if it goes away — whatever "it" is, then it is almost always a demon controlling that area of the person's life and thinking.

Physical manifestations might happen if they get agitated while you are praying for them. They might begin to do one or more of these things: wring their hands, get a headache, become very nervous, blank out, their eyes change (might actually roll back in their head), or they might begin to make noises. Demons might cause the person to make a whimpering sound. It's so you will feel sorry for them and stop because you think it's coming from the person instead of a demonic spirit manifesting. They might be trying to intimidate you.

If you are praying for someone who begins to exhibit these manifestations, remember to be loving and kind in how you speak to the person while being firm with the evil spirit who is behind it. Spirits don't have a problem hearing you, so you don't need to shout.

Remember that every thought one has doesn't necessarily originate with them, so if you reject those that don't line up with scripture and who God says you are, you'll have victory in those areas of deception. For example: You are inadequate, unloved, rejected, stupid, not worthy, etc. — are all clearly lies.

Discussion:

If demons don't announce their presence, how would you recognize it if you or others are dealing with a demon?

💗 Thoughts suggested by the enemy are not yours until you agree by accepting them as true. We always have a choice (1 Thessalonians 2:18).

Demons want to hinder us as Christians from doing God's will. (Read *The Screwtape Letters,* by C.S. Lewis). Demons use a person's mind and personality, wanting to express their demonic emotions through that person's body.

When something important is about to happen in your life, you will usually come under attack and want to give up. You will start believing lies and think you are not effective and that what you do doesn't matter or isn't good enough; you aren't good enough, etc. It is up to you whether or not that emotion controls your mind and body. As we touched on earlier, just because you don't "feel" like reaching out to someone doesn't mean you shouldn't do it. Your mind and spirit will be at war, and you won't want to be inconvenienced. This is when you need to crucify your flesh. You shouldn't "reason" your way out of it. Ask the Holy Spirit to empower you.

 **God Moment:**

Close your eyes and listen…

Dear one, I have brought you to a new threshold. It's up to you if you go through. There are things I want to show you. There are new gifts I have for you to receive. But you have to be willing to take a risk and trust Me that I have your best interest in mind.

There is a whole new realm you haven't experienced, so I want to take you deeper; don't be afraid. Surrender to Me and to My will for your life.

Ezekiel 47:1

Psalm 42:7

Assignment:

How has Satan attacked your mind?

_____
_____
_____

How did that affect your emotions?

_____
_____
_____

How did your behavior change?

_____
_____
_____

Final thought:

Truth always leads to freedom and lies will always lead to bondage.

Journal:

Lesson 9: Dangerous Open Doors

I hope you understand by now that spiritual warfare is real and has roots that go back farther than the Garden of Eden; that there is an active spiritual realm that exists that we cannot see. But you are not powerless in the battle between good and evil. You have authority based on your position in Christ. However, I can't emphasize enough how so many things that are accepted as "harmless" in our modern culture are absolutely not harmless and have long-standing roots in evil, as well as long-term consequences. Consider carefully the following ways you can inadvertantly open a door for Satan.

Open doors that make it possible for Satan to influence or dominate a Christian:

- Fortune telling, palm reading, astrology (belief that your birth sign of the Zodiac influences your destiny). If you go to a fortuneteller and submit to and come into agreement with them, you are opening the door for a curse in your life. An example would be having them tell you that you are going to have heart trouble, and then you do. *(That happened to a friend of mine as a result of believing what the psychic said.)*

- Mediums are now actually saying they are channeling people's pets so the person can know what their animal is thinking and feeling! (This happened with talk show host Kelly Rippa's dog on her TV show.) These imposters always use just enough truth to get the hook in.

- Using Ouija boards, séances, clairvoyance, any mind-expanding drugs, or charms to ward off spirits or bring "good" luck.

- Extra Sensory Perception (ESP), transcendental meditation (TM, which stems from Hinduism), soul travel, and astral projection.

When our son was a teenager, we had a young man come live with us who was about twenty-one years old. He was a college student who was having mental issues, and his parents, who were divorced, didn't know what to do. Our pastor asked if we would take him in and try to help him. It turns out he had been deeply into transcendental meditation and had been practicing astral projection. He had become a Christian because the last time he had an out of body experience, he had trouble getting back into his body. It frightened him so much that he began searching for truth and came to know Christ. However, it also caused a lot of emotional issues for him, mostly based in fear and insecurity.

Call it white magic or black magic — both open a door for the demonic to enter.

Once there was a lady I'd never met before who came to the small group that met in our home. She stood next to me during the worship, and I heard the Lord say that she has demons. This surprised me because she looked fine to me, but the thought stayed with me, so when we had a break I quietly asked her if she knew what evil spirits were. She immediately said, "Oh yes, that's why I'm here; I was a witch, but now I'm a Christian. I'm still tormented, however, and I need help to be free." We told the group, and then began to pray over her. The demons left with loud screaming, and she was completely free.

- Tarot cards, channeling crystals, divination, or fire-walking, which is sometimes practiced by the Unitarian church.

One holiday our family was visiting other family members for several days. After being there overnight, my daughter told me the next morning that she had not been able to sleep all night. She wanted me to look at a picture on the wall over the bed where she was staying because she thought it was demonic. So I went to look, and it was of two female goddesses in an intimate pose. I prayed about what to say or do because these were people I cared for deeply, and I knew something in their lives was very wrong. Later that day when only our family was left, I asked the teenager whose room it was about the picture. I told her what was wrong with it and actually shared the gospel with her and explained that it was an open door that allowed Satan into her life. She is a very shy person and didn't really want to say much about it, but I could tell she was upset (this was not a family of believers at the time). She politely listened, then went into her mother's room and shut the door. The mother followed her in, and they were in there for a while, so I wasn't sure what was going on. But when the mother came out, she told me that the daughter wouldn't sleep in her room, and instead, slept with her every night. As a result of what I had said about the picture, she admitted to her mother that the reason she wouldn't sleep in her room was because there was "a woman" who came into her room every night doing things around her room, and it frightened her. When the mother told us what the daughter had said, I asked her if she, the mother, also had things in her possession that would be an open door to the enemy. She brought out her Tarot cards and mentioned a few other things. Because they were frightened, they were willing to get rid of everything. Once they did, the teenager was able to sleep peacefully in her own room.

- Some music truly is inspired by evil (Stevie Nick's recording studio is called Wicca).

- Horoscopes (charts to predict destiny).
- Internet or tabletop games that glorify evil, violence, and the occult.

Years ago a mother brought her son to our church to have prayer for deliverance from a demonic spirit. He had been heavily into a popular role-playing game that often featured occult content and was experiencing a lot of behavioral problems. When we began to pray for him, he began to slither across the floor like a snake, and his pupils actually turned into slits shaped like a snake's. Unfortunately, I'm not sure he ever found freedom.

- Hypnotism can be an open door for evil spirits as you give up control of your own mind.
- Incubus (an evil spirit that sexually violates a woman) and Succubus (an evil spirit in a woman's form that seduces men) spirits.

I once prayed with a woman who thought her ex-boyfriend's spirit was visiting her at night to have sex. She actually felt what she thought was his touch and had a physical response to it.

- Kaballah, a Jewish mystical tradition that is based on a mathematical interpretation of scripture, resulting in various magical and occult practices.
- Levitation, Silva mind control, mind reading, mysticism (emptying your mind so you can attain spiritual union with the ultimate reality, necromancy, New Age movement, numerology).
- Masons practice modern paganism. It uses the same initiation as the initiate goes through in witchcraft or in the Satanist

Church. All of the rituals of the Freemasons are identical, except the signature of the pagan, druid, or witch must be signed in human blood. The rituals of Freemasonry are directed to the sun god Ra and are mysterious pagan practices that are highly secretive. The beliefs are founded in the Baal/Peor worship, the god Molach, and other mysterious deities. The initiates soon learn that they have obligations. When they reach the various degrees of power, they find that requirements must be kept, and they vow to keep them secret. The vows and the consequences if you break them extend to your family members as well. They actually take a vow to Lucifer called the Luciferan Doctrine at the 30th, 31th, and 32nd degree.[5]

- Telekinesis, controlling objects with the mind, parapsychology, pentagram, psychic healing, psychometric- holding an object belonging to someone and gaining knowledge about them.

- Reincarnation, Satanism, sorcery, "spiritism" (summoning demons), spirit guides, stigmata (that is, manifestations of bodily wounds, scars and pain in locations corresponding to the crucifixion wounds of Jesus Christ, such as the hands, wrists, and feet), as well as superstitions, tea-leaf reading, third-eye, and telekinesis.

- Voodoo, which is religious witchcraft.

- Hatha Yoga, in the Hindu religion it's the path followed to realize god within you; a spiritual discipline aimed at controlling the physical, spiritual and psychic; the aim is to awaken the kundalini power of the serpent lying dormant at the base of the spine.

[5] *See Appendix A for more information and help.*

- Communicating with the dead is forbidden in scripture, yet it is becoming a popular practice. People want assurance that there is an afterlife; they want to know their loved ones are in some kind of heaven. Many loved ones who are left behind have unresolved issues, so they try to talk to the departed looking for some kind of closure. Perhaps they are stuck in the grieving process or lonely, so when the enemy appears disguised as the person they want to contact, they are ready to be deceived into believing it's true. *Dr. Oz* and the *Today Show* have had these mediums on their show, supposedly channeling the dead. In 2 Corinthians 11:14 Paul says Satan has the power to masquerade as an angel of light. He will present himself as God (or anyone else) in order to deceive.

As evangelicals we are not exempt; Satan can cause us to be religious through self-effort and superstition. Author Tim Keller gives a good example.

> *Religions operate on the principle: "I obey, therefore I am accepted," but the gospel principle is: "I am accepted through Christ, therefore I obey." So the gospel differs from both irreligion and religion. You can seek to be your own "lord and savior" by breaking the law of God, but you can also do so by keeping the law in order to earn your salvation. Religion and secularism tend to inflate self–encouraging, uncritical, "self–esteem;" religion and moralism crush people under guilt from ethical standards that are impossible to maintain. The gospel, however, humbles and affirms us at the same time, since, in Christ, each of us is simultaneously just and a sinner still. At the same time, we are more flawed and sinful than we ever dared believe, yet we are more loved and accepted than we ever dared hope."*
> – *Gospel Coaltion,* Tim Keller and D. A. Carson

Physical acts in spiritual warfare

Physical acts can parallel the establishing of spiritual authority. A physical act can become a symbol of a reality that impacts the invisible as action is being taken in the invisible realm. For example, when we take holy communion, or are baptised, something happens in the spiritual realm in tandem with the physical act. The same is true of other spiritual expressions such as prayer, standing, kneeling, dancing, fasting, raising hands in praise, worship, etc. These actions address the invisible realm, and as a result, gain victories (Acts 6:1-4; Jeremiah 29:11-14).

- Hezekiah spread a letter to petition the Lord in 2 Kings 19:14-19, 35; (which is also told in Isaiah 37:14-20, 36).
- Vocal praise and shouting (1 Samuel 4:5-6; 1 Kings 1:40).
- Lifting hands and bowing heads (Nehemiah 8:6).
- Dancing or leaping (Psalm 149:3; Luke 6:23).
- Groaning in prayer (Romans 8:23; Galatians 4:19).
- Shaking or trembling (Acts 16:29; Hebrews 12:21).
- Intense weeping (Ezra 3:13; Lamentations 1:16, 20).
- Prostrating yourself before the Lord (Ezekiel 1:26-28; Matthew 17:6; Acts 9:1-9, 10:9-14).

Physical things can carry spiritual significance.

Likewise, physical things can carry spiritual significance by providing access to demonic spirits. They can be a point of contact for use by demonic spirits, and they are used to gain spiritual power. They are an invitation for demons to enter a home.

Forbidden things in scripture.
- Worship of other gods (Exodus 20:3).
- Figures of idols of other countries (1 Corinthians 8:5).
- Astrology/fortune telling (Deuteronomy 18:10).
- Witchcraft/sorcery (Galatians 5:20-21).
- Necromancy (Leviticous 20:27).

These practices open the door to supernatural deception, hinder spiritual and physical health, and cause a turning from God. They will also dull your spiritual senses and weaken your conscience (1 Corinthians 8:7).

Discussion:

Have you ever worn anything for protection? Was it from legalism or being superstitious?

Cults.

All cults are based on doctrinal errors, misinterpretation or misapplication of scripture. Below are a few:
- Animism (believing that inanimate things like plant, trees, stones have a life and spirit of their own).
- Buddhism, Hinduism, Islam (all worship other gods).
- Jehovah's Witness (deny the deity of Jesus, believe archangel Michael was Jesus in his pre-human state).
- Mormonism (They believe you must marry in a Mormon temple to achieve godhood in eternity; they baptize for the dead.) Reformed Mormon church is the same but doesn't practice polygamy or baptism for the dead.

- Scientology (believe there are many gods, no such thing as sin or evil, and that hell is a myth).
- Unitarian Universalist (believe in one God but teach that Orthodox Christianity has forsaken the real, human Jesus and seek to promote harmony between all faiths, reject doctrine of the Trinity and virgin birth, and the belief that Jesus is the Messiah and God Incarnate.).

Four ways to recognize deception:
1. Adding to the Bible and saying that other books hold equal weight. (*The Book of Mormon* and *Divine Principle* from the Unitarian church.)
2. Subtracting from the person of Christ. (The Jehovah Witnesses teach that Jesus is a created being, not part of the Trinity, God the Creator.)
3. Works to earn salvation. (Conditions of special ceremonies, or adhering to non-Biblical beliefs.)
4. Dividing loyalties of the followers. (Teaching to trust in organizations or a person leading.)

Emotional extremes of triumph or disaster can also cause us to be vulnerable to the enemy. Our life in Christ should always be mobile: forward and upward, never stagnant. To remain free from bondage, a person has to break the legal partnership with the enemy. Repentance closes the door to the enemy. Forgiveness may be required, but you also have to be willing to part with and destroy whatever is still in your possession.

Since Freemasonry is a cult, you should get rid of any jewelry or artifacts connected to the practice. (You can get the book from their Lodge to read information regarding the oaths and curses.)

Prayer for repentance leading to freedom: *Lord, I repent for myself and on behalf of my ancestors for opening the door to the enemy because of the following practices: _____. I ask for and receive your forgiveness. I renounce them and I ask you to remove any spiritual darkness over my mind, my body, my home, and my family as a result of these wrong beliefs and practices. I command every spirit of darkness associated with these objects and cults to leave me in the name of Jesus. I ask you to fill those places with the fruit of the Spirit. Thank you for hearing my prayer and delivering me. Amen* **(Galatians 5:22).**

Other manifestations of and open doors to evil spirits.

Addictions (all kinds)

    Emotional = overeating; self-harm

    Sexual = homosexuality, pornography

Thoughts/Beliefs

    Legalism

    Spiritual bondage

    Escapism (the enemy doesn't want you to receive ministry so you will have the urge to leave);

    Deceitful personality from fear of punishment from parents or others

    Shame

Behavior and Mental Issues

    Extremes: Torments, such as uncontrollable obsessive compulsive behavior, or similar extreme behaviors involving fear/paranoia, anger, anxiety, depression, unforgiveness, jealousy, guilt, self-condemnation, hearing voices

Violence

Irrational Behavior: control/domination, nightmares

Suicidal tendencies

Withdrawn/anti-social

Self-centeredness

Health Issues

Heredity Illnesses

Appetite out of balance

More doors that give legal access:

(*We will expound on this more later*)

- Ancestral sins and curses (familiar spirits that manifest through strong tendencies of violence, physical infirmities, insanity, controlling desires, addictions, depression, alcoholism, other repetitive problems within the family line.)
- Unforgiveness
- Willful disobedience
- Emotional trauma
- Inner vows and judgments (These cause the generational sin to be locked in and repeated.)
- Soul ties
- Word curses – when we believe them and agree with them
- Anger
- Pent up emotions

Primary Causes that might open doors to the enemy.

- Rebellion and disrespect for parents (Ephesians 6:1-3).
- Acknowledging and worshipping false gods (Exodus 20:103).
- Involvement with the occult (Deuteronomy 27:17).
- Iniquity and oppression (Deuteronomy 27:17-19).
- All forbidden, aberrant, or unlawful sexual relationships (Deuteronomy 27:20-23).
- Anti-Semitism (Genesis 12:3).
- Dependence upon human strength, wisdom and goodness (Jeremiah 17:5-6).
- Stealing and lying (Zechariah 5:3-4).
- Withholding tithes and offerings (Malachi 3:8-9).
- Words spoken by those in authority - curses instead of blessings (Genesis 31:32).
- Negative idle words spoken about yourself (Matthew 12:36-37).
- Oaths or covenants taken for admission to secret societies and ungodly organizations (Exodus 23:32).
- Curses that are pronounced by witches, warlocks, other occultist activity (Ezekiel 13:17-23).
- Damaging slanderous words directed against others for harm (James 3:14-15).
- Manipulating prayers that seek to control others, inacting your will instead of God's will (Proverbs 28:9).
- Wrong desires (James 1:15).

Emotional involvement could make you susceptible to the enemy.

Peter seemed to be most tuned in to the spirit realm compared to the other disciples. He had a revelation of who Jesus was in Matthew 16:16-17, yet he allowed Satan to speak through him in Matthew 16:21-23 when he told Jesus not to go to the cross. He understood who and what Jesus was, yet what he wanted in the flesh, emotionally, overcame the Spirit.

He did it again on the Mount of Transfiguration when he wanted to build a tabernacle to prolong the experience (Matthew 17). We can't "set up camp" on one experience. Building a tabernacle on the mountain and not moving on to the cross would be a lifeless form of religion based on one experience instead of the Blood of Jesus. Also, we cannot interpret one experience as the gospel — many today leave out the experience of the cross completely. Lifeless religion is what happens when we try to live on past experiences or on someone else's experience and not intimately know Christ for ourselves.

Willful sin opens the door to the enemy.

If people open the door to the enemy and *willingly* keep it open, you have no authority over the enemy in their life. However, if they themselves don't have willful sin in their life but are being abused by an evil spirit or another person, then God may speak through you to free him/her by taking spiritual authority over it when the Holy Spirit reveals it to you. An example would be when I was praying for people after speaking at a women's retreat. *There was a young woman attending whose husband was abusive. I had never met her, so I didn't know anything about her relationship with her husband until God spoke through me and said "no more." I saw her years later, and she told me that he never hit her again after that night. In fact, he began to treat her like a princess.*

> Through prayer, we touch heaven and change earth.

Abortion can open the door to a tormenting spirit.

If you have ever had an abortion, please consider to going to a Deeper Still Retreat (or similar ministry) where you can experience freedom from the guilt and shame associated with abortion. You can contact Jacque Murphy at:

Jacque.Murphy@GoDeeperStill.org

for more information. There is no charge for the weekend retreat.

Demonic entry points.

1. Generational line
2. Personal sin and rebellion
3. Occult sin (Masonic oaths)
4. Some alternative medical practices
5. Religious sin (praying to saints/idols)
6. Ungodly soul ties
7. Sexual sin (demonic powers attach to sexual sin)
8. Abuse, hurts, rejection
9. Traumas and accidents
10. Death
11. Curses
12. Cursed objects
13. Addictions
14. Fears
15. Fatigue and tiredness (these can also be caused by witchcraft)
16. Deceitful personality and behavior (this can begin early in life from fear of punishment by parents)

There are ranks of authority in the spirit realm.

It appears that there are *ranks of authority* in the heavenly angelic realm, and the same seems true for the evil angelic realm of demons (Ephesians 6:12).

The Ephesians scripture gives a picture of four divisions in the demonic realm (rulers, authorities, cosmic powers, and present darkness). The exact hierarchical relationship between these terms is unclear. Some seem to derive from human conceptions of geographical rule and political power. New Testament writers, especially Paul, draw on this worldview that we see reflected in the book of Daniel, Chapter 10, where nations are under the authority of angelic princes. Colossians 1:16 seems to also refer to divine rulers. Our translations of "rulers" and "principalities" are usually from the Greek term *arche* and *archon*. In scripture they may refer to either human or divine.

Perhaps the divisions look like this:

- Territorial demons:

Principalities would be forces/gods that appear to have dominion over nations and governments. The *Septuagint*, which is the oldest translation of the Jewish scriptures (our Old Testament) from the original Hebrew language, uses the term *sar*, meaning "prince." When a principality was defined, a prince or god was set over it (Daniel 10:13, 20; 12:1). The ruling princes over the nations became corrupt. Yet they remain in power, and are authorized to use as many demons as necessary from all orders and ranks to perform Satan's work in that specified principality/geographical area to which they've been assigned. Examples would include the spirits of perversion, homosexuality, poverty, power, oppression as is exhibited in dictatorships; we can also see the influence of spirits behind other dictators, and those that tend to rule over a nation, state, or city. We can intercede and ask God to pull down those demonic strongholds.

- *Powers (cosmic):* Powers denote force, capability, and potency. It does not denote any specific rank. Powers have authority and power of action in the entire sphere or region that is given to them. It appears they are lords over certain places.

- *Rulers of darkness:* These govern the thinking of the world at large. They seem to be the most intelligent type of spirits. I don't think our authority extends to this realm (however, we can intercede and ask God to break that demonic rule). Our authority would extend to the spirits personally tormenting an individual.

- *Spiritual forces of evil:* Demons (Satan's minions) that attack individuals are known as *strongman, legion, pride, anger, incest, ruler, chief,* or have no name but have specific functions. They might be assigned to situations to cause trouble (Ephesians 6:12; Romans 8:38). This is in the realm of the first heaven, and our authority extends over them.

- *Thrones and authorities:* Colossians 1:16 also contains two other terms of rank and power called *thronos* and *exousia*. These are usually translated "thrones" and "authorities." These terms refer to some sphere of authority and the ability to rule that sphere. *Exousia* is most frequently used in the New Testament for the right to use power bestowed upon someone by an office. Ephesians 1:21, 3:10, and Colossians 2:10 use this term, *exousia*, to refer to divine beings. This is likely connected to the worldview in Deuteronomy 32:8-9.

Satan was an Archangel; he is a religious and political personality.

Since he cannot be everywhere at once, he must dispatch chief rulers (principalities) to guard and protect his perverted schemes for empires, nations, states, and cities. Scripture says he is *the prince of the power of the air*. He wants control of the world's political, religious, and economic structures. When you understand this, it's easier to understand how the minds of our media, Hollywood, and government have been so influenced by the realm of darkness.

The demons disguised as gods are more attractive to man than those who actually do the influencing or possessing. They influence and control man's thinking about life in a certain way. Then when a person begins to act on that belief system, they take dominion in that area. The other kind of demonic spirits actually enter in to live in a person and use his body.

Discussion:

Is it hard to believe the demonic realm is organized and has ranks of demon spirits? Do you think those higher up in the ranks are fallen angels? Why?

The bottom line is that evil spirits are on the earth and want to influence and oppress mankind. They want a body to inhabit so they can be most influential working through people. When we dabble in the wrong realm of the supernatural, no matter how innocent, we open the door to these forces of darkness. We can come under Satan's influence and power (Leviticus 19:31).

God Moment:

Close your eyes and listen . . .

Beloved, don't be afraid of what you don't understand. I am bigger than all of it. Don't be overwhelmed by circumstances. I'm in control when you hand it over to Me and trust Me. I've got your back; don't fear, lean into Me.

Allow Me to handle those things that are too hard and overwhelming for you. Hand Me the burdens you carry for others. They are not meant for you.

My yoke is easy, and My burden is light. Be yoked to Me and let Me lead you. I will take you in the direction you need to go.

Matthew 11:30

Galatians 6:2

Assignment:

Ask the Lord to reveal any deception in your life and write down what you think He is saying.

_____
_____

What is the enemy's strategy against you?

_____
_____

How has Satan controlled you through patterns of wrong thinking?

_____
_____

Ask the Holy Spirit if you have allowed the enemy to destroy any relationships in your life. What was the open door and what sin was involved?

_____
_____

Describe a time when your thoughts triggered emotional turmoil and how it affected your body.

_____
_____

Final Thought:

Deliverance is a beginning process, not an "end all."

Journal:

Lesson 10: Distinguishing Angels from Demons

You may have heard the cliché around Christian circles that, "although we're not to judge others, we are fruit inspectors," referring to the fruits of the spirit vs. the fruits of the flesh. But many Christians, new and mature alike, go through periods of time when they wonder, are they hearing from God or someone else? Looking at spiritual fruit is actually a pretty good place to start. Here are some ways we can determine if we're hearing from God or from the enemy, based on the result or "fruit" involved.

If you battle one of these groupings, it usually means you have opened the door for those listed under each heading. Sometimes the characteristics are the same but attached to a different stronghold, such as anger with hate, but hate opened the door for anger. Likewise, depression attaches to a spirit of heaviness, and condemnation attaches to both shame and heaviness.

Demonic groupings and demonic attachments[6].

Anger
    Bitterness
    Resentment
    Depression
    Revenge
    Sometimes rage

Pride
    Ungrateful, Materialistic
    Mocking, Self-righteous
    Stubborn
    Sarcastic, Competitive
    Impatient

---

[6] See Workbook 5, *Healing Prayer*, for more information

Shame/Blame, Lies
> Guilt
>
> Deception
>
> Lying spirits *(Their assignment is to cause you to hold onto the shame)*

Fear
> Worry, Inferiority, Insecurity, Perfectionism
>
> Anxiety, Timidity
>
> Panic, Phobias, fear of failure

Rejection
> Abandonment, Withdrawal
>
> Neglect, Loneliness, Jealousy
>
> Insecurity, Addictive behavior
>
> Compulsions

Confusion
> Doubt, Unbelief
>
> Suspicion, Skeptical
>
> Nervous, Distorted judgment
>
> Indecisive/Double-minded

Hate
> Cutting, Piercing, excessive tattooing
>
> Anger, Self-hatred
>
> Murder

Lust
> Pornography, Perversion
>
> Fantasy
>
> Adultery, Incest, Homosexuality

Death
- Suicide
- Death wish
- Infirmity
- Anorexia
- Bulimia
- Alcoholism
- Nicotine
- Drugs

Heaviness
- Depression
- Despair
- Self-pity
- Suicidal thoughts
- Unconfessed sin
- Condemnation

Occult spirits
- New age, Ouija boards
- Palm reading
- Fortune telling
- Cults
- Séances
- Religious spirits (*Free Masonry, Scientology, Mormonism, Islam, Buddhism*)

Control
- Witchcraft
- Confusion
- Fatigue

Demons do not want Christians to have the fruit or the gifts of the Spirit evident in their lives. If you have a spirit of resentment or rejection, you will find it hard to love yourself or others. A spirit of resentment will open the door for other spirits like unforgiveness, bitterness, and anger. A spirit of rejection will open the door for other spirits like unworthiness and insecurity. A spirit of shame will open the door for self-hatred and ugliness. Bitterness is usually rooted in unforgiveness, anger, and resentment. The truth about your true identity in Christ brings freedom.

Symptoms of demonic groupings on a personal level.

A spirit of infirmity can cause physical weakness, allergies, heart trouble, and female problems. Always make sure there isn't a natural cause like a nutritional issue or other natural causes. If there isn't a natural cause, look for a spiritual root.

With a stronghold of rejection, you will usually find fear of rejection by others as well as self-rejection. Someone with a spirit of rejection will make you want to reject him or her. The fear of rejection will cause them to do something to make you reject them if you are not aware of what's going on. Even then it's hard to accept them. Self-rejection comes in because they begin to agree with the enemy that there is something wrong with them, so then self-hatred comes in too. They exude rejection. When you see a kid with *excessive* piercings and tattoos, there is likely a spirit of rejection on them.

Demons don't want humans to receive truth or to be delivered because then they have to find another body through which to accomplish their purpose, which is to manifest through their host feelings of rejection, pride, hate, anger, murder, perversion, and so forth. They will do anything to steal your identity and destroy it.

In Matthew 12:43 the demon referred to the person's body as his house. But scripture says we Christians are the temple of the Holy Spirit, so they have no legal right to be there; they are trespassing. For this reason they try to remain hidden and not be obvious to the person being oppressed or to the one praying for them. They will also try to appeal to your sentiments in order to stay.

The man in Mark 5:2-15 whose body was completely controlled by demon spirits is an example of being demonized. He had no control over his actions and had been demonized for a long time. He lived like a sub-human living between the decaying and dead. He had no dignity and was violent. He had supernatural strength, was tormented and self-destructive with cutting. His behavior was uncontrollable. What people saw was not who he really was because his soul was imprisoned, and his miserable existence was caused by the demons. But even so, when the man saw Jesus, he was able to worship Him. The one that spoke to Jesus was one of the invading spirits. A superstition of that day was that if you used the person's precise name, it would give you power over them. However, the demons used the name Legion, which at that time, would be about 6,000 men in the Roman army, so it might have been an intimidation tactic showing that there were thousands of them.

The only way the soul of that man could be helped was from outside intervention. Someone had to cast out the demons because at that point, he could not help himself.

There is a difference between demonic visitation and demonic habitation. The pigs may have run off the cliff because they couldn't stand the demonic spirits. Jesus may have allowed the demons to enter the pigs because pigs were considered unclean. Jews were not supposed to eat them or raise them because it was illegal under the Mosaic Law. Demons are assigned to or have simply decided to dwell in certain geographic locations; they don't want to leave. Perhaps that's another reason they wanted to go into the pigs.

Another example is in the movie, *Lord of the Rings, Two Towers*.

King Theodan in *Lord of the Rings* could not help himself. He had become taken over by a spirit of witchcraft from Saruman, who was likely being controlled by a demonic principality over that region. Saruman wanted to take over and rule the region. The king's oppression was obvious when you looked at his eyes. We see Grema (which means *worm tongue*), who had a lying spirit whispering things in the king's ear to deceive him, causing him to be suspicious of others. It kept him in bondage by poisoning his mind. He couldn't make choices on his own because he wasn't in his right mind. We see the enemy working from both the outside and the inside. Notice how unclean he appears, how dirty his nails are, how weak and complacent he is, and how much he has aged. The demon speaks out of the king to challenge Gandolf's authority. The king says his dreams have become dark of late. (Nightmares can be a sign of oppression.)

He needed help from outside himself. He needed someone who had and understood spiritual authority to intercede on his behalf. When Gandolf steps in to free him, it is not Theodan's physical being that is cast onto the floor, but it is the demon controlling him. When the ruling demon is gone, he becomes free. His strength returns, and he is given his sword, which represents a position of authority to rule over the kingdom. He is free to make the right choices.

Gollum in *Lord of the Rings* appears to be possessed by a demon. He was once a Hobbit named Smeagol. He certainly doesn't appear as a normal Hobbit or human. *(Oddly enough, while ministering to people with actual demonic spirits, I've had them speak to me in voices that sounded identical to this.)*

Sam sees Gollum for who and what he really is: a liar and a deceiver. Frodo thinks he can save him and wants his freedom more than Gollum himself wants it. Smeagol killed for the ring because he was so greedy for power and position. He began to live in a cave and feared the light. He is a good example of what happens when we invite demons in by acting on temptation. He called the ring "my precious," and it ruled him.

While I'm not saying there's a demon behind every bush, if you look at our culture, particularly movies and video games, you'll see the clear presence of demonic spirits, witchcraft, and the occult. These concepts are often taught or presented to our children as harmless. They are not.

Remember, there is a difference between demonic visitation and demonic habitation

The enemy uses lies, suspicion of others, and deception to keep us in bondage. We have been given a place of spiritual authority to rule over spiritual darkness in the kingdom of God, but if we listen to the lies being whispered in our ear, we will become powerless to use it. The enemy will arrange circumstances to support his lies, which will cause us to believe the worst about people. He tries to manipulate our thoughts, feelings, and actions based on his agenda, not what is actually true.

The current trend is living transgender lifestyles, at younger and younger ages, and calling it normal. The thinking is that you can decide which sex you want to be today. Your gender can change with your mood. I believe it's a result of demonic spirits influencing a person's thinking. The body will follow the dictates of the mind, and feelings will then line up with both resulting in a demonic stronghold that feels very real.

Some people have lived their lives in agreement with demon spirits; they don't want to change because they fear losing their identity. Examples could be an actual spirit of academia (intellectualism), control, self-sufficiency, hate, unforgiveness, ritualism, gender deception, or other disruptive spirit. James 4:7 says if we draw near to God and resist, the enemy will flee. The original Greek actually says *he will flee in terror*.

Satan has limited knowledge and can't be omnipresent.

How the enemy (Satan) gains entrance through open doors that give legal access:

- He tempts us to deceive us.
- He tempts us to act independent from God (Matthew 4).
- He tempts us to desire his power and rule (Luke 4).
- He accuses us and causes false guilt.
- Intrusion or sin that comes through:
    - Lies and deception.
    - Accusation and condemnation.
    - Doubt, fear, and unbelief.
    - Battle for the mind – torment and obsession.
    - Attacking the validity of the Word of God.

When we give ground to any of these, we're giving territory to demon spirits. Coming into agreement with any of his lies, deceptions, or mis-directions gives an open door to Satan.

Who the devil cannot deceive, he tries to destroy; whom he cannot destroy, he attempts to deceive.

Prayer to bind the enemy from operating against you through someone you are talking with: *"In the name of Jesus, I take authority over the spirit of strife, anger, rage, criticism, accusing, or meanness* (whatever is coming against you), *and I command you to stop right now. I command you to be silent in my presence in the name of Jesus."*

A simple solution and spiritual weapon against the enemy is worship (Psalm 22:3). When we praise the Lord, He becomes enthroned on our praises, and as a result the power of the enemy over us is broken. Satan will leave when we worship the Lord because he has no power in the presence of God. Praise and worship brings us closer to God and empowers us; it changes the climate, and Satan has to leave. If that is hard for you to do, ask the Holy Spirit to begin to worship through you.

If you have never asked Jesus to come into your heart and be Lord of your life, pray this prayer: *Lord Jesus, I repent of my sins and ask for your salvation. Come live in me and create a new heart within me. I thank you for making me a new creature and filling me with the Holy Spirit. Amen*

God Moment

Close your eyes and listen…

Put on some worship music, and as you listen to the words begin to worship Me in your heart. As you focus on Me, I will begin to speak to you. The darkness over you will be dispelled.

My thoughts toward you are good and loving. My love for you never ends. No power can stop My goodness and kindness toward you, so stop doubting My love and faithfulness. My love never fails. It is bigger than your circumstances.

Jeremiah 29:11; Jeremiah 31:3 Isaiah 54:10

Assignment:

Ask God if there is an open door in your life to the enemy, and write your answer below.

_____
_____

What do you think the scripture, "give the devil an opportunity" means?

_____
_____

How does anger become fertile ground for demonic activity?

_____
_____

Final thought:

Submit yourselves therefore to God, resist the devil and he will flee from you (James 4:7).

Lesson 11: Align Your Will with God's

Satan is not anti-religion, but he is anti-Christ

The enemy doesn't mind religion as long as a person's motive and heart are not in the right place. He will assign a religious spirit to the person and use it to dominate them. This is especially true when someone isn't a believer but is just going through the motions. With believers, it happens when their focus is not on the Lord but on themselves and their performance. When they have no relationship with the Lord, they have no revelation of grace. This can lead to frustration, torment, anxiety, and pent-up anger. It could ultimately result in rage, which will surface in certain situations that trigger the emotions, releasing what has been building up. You can be sure the lid will come off under the right circumstances. It will look and feel like a volcano when the pressure hits the right point. There will be an eruption and an uncalled-for level of intensity. Unfortunately, it will lead to legalism and eventually open the door to sin and bondage, involving pride and frustration.

Personal sin attracts demons

Spiritual atmosphere has to do with attitudes and behaviors. When a person exudes bad attitudes and behaviors, the spiritual atmosphere around them will literally attract demonic spirits. For example, we saw in the last lesson how anger invites hate, malice, bitterness, rage, jealousy, and resentment. These spirits can permeate a home, business, or relationship.

Since most sins are rooted in pride, when we walk in humility it dispels the darkness. Being filled with the fruit of the Spirit (Galatians 5:22-26) will repel demons and dispel the darkness.

Discussion:

Have you ever seen anyone delivered from a demonic spirit or known of anyone who was? How were they changed?

Jesus said Satan had no place in Him (John 14:30), so be determined not to let him have a place in you either. Make sure you keep your heart right before God and toward others. Do not give the enemy a foothold (legal right) in your mind or life (Ephesians 4:27). Deliberate sin will give him access to your mind and body.

We recognize demonic influence by:

- Discerning of spirits (remember, this is not suspicion; discerning of spirits comes from your spirit by the Holy Spirit while suspicion comes from your mind and usually begins with doubt)
- Detection - observing what they do to a person (not the same as mentally struggling with a temptation)
- Recognizing repetitive behavior that could indicate generational demonic problems

For more detail on recognizing demonic influence, see Appendix B.

Names reflect character:

Our actions and attitudes eventually change our character — who we are at our very core. Biblical names reflect character. Joseph, a Levite who sold land and gave the money to the apostles, became known as Barnabas, "son of encouragement." *Rebellion* will change your character, and in turn, who you are. Satan was called Lucifer in Isaiah 14:12, which in Latin means, "shining one," or "Day Star, Son of Dawn," and represented the planet Venus. This reflects who God created him to be, but Jesus called him Satan in

Luke 10:18, meaning "adversary, opposer," because that's who he became[7]. When we rebel against God, our very nature changes.

Names of Satan that reflect position:

- Anointed cherub who covers - Exekiel 28:14
    Cherub had three roles: (1) to guard the source of life (Genesis 3:24); (2) to draw the chariot of God (Psalm 18:10, 2 Samuel 22:11, Ezekiel 1:5-20, 10:1-22); (3) to serve as the throne for God over the Mercy Seat (1 Kings 6:23, 8:6-8). In Ezekiel 28:14 an "anointed cherub" functioned as a guardian within the garden of Eden.
- Prince of this world - John 12:31; 16:11.
- Prince of power of the Air - Ephesians 2:2.
- God of this Age - 2 Corinthians 4:4.
- Prince of Demons - Matthew 12:24; Luke 11:15.

Names of Satan that reflect character.

Lucifer

Satan

Devil

Old Serpent

Great Dragon

Evil One

Destroyer

Tempter

Accuser

Deceiver

Spirit who now works in Sons of Disobedience

---

[7] *See Appendix C for more detail.*

Wrong desires lead to deception and disobedience, as in the story of David and Bathsheba. Sometimes wrong desires meet a good need in a bad way. For example, food is necessary and good, but not when desire for it grows into gluttony; sex was created as a gift from God to be enjoyed within marriage, but outside of marriage, it is wrong; likewise, sleep can become laziness, exercise can be either useful or prideful, and so forth. Desires become wrong when they control you, rather than the other way around.

Our sovereign will is important.

God gave us a will so we can make moral choices. Demons take over a person because he/she has willfully given permission, usually through deception or deliberate sin of some kind. When this happens, it becomes a legal tie, and contract rights are given to the demonic. As a result, demons can inhabit a place or person, and it requires deliverance to evict them. It is important to identify the offense that was committed, destroy the contracts made with darkness, and remove the things that seal, symbolize, attract, and enable darkness. Then close the door — dedicate the home/person to the Lord.

There is power when your will aligns with God's.

Be careful about the jewelry you purchase, especially when traveling. When you go to another country, be careful about your choice of souvenirs. For example, in Egypt don't purchase a necklace with the image of Nefertiti's head. Don't buy a carving of her head. You don't want in your possession a statue of Buddha or of any other foreign thing or person worshipped in another culture. When traveling, don't bring back objects symbolizing gods worshipped by tribes or American Indians, or pictures portraying any of that. These objects are particularly prevelent in Africa, and certain areas of the western United States, and the deep South. If you bring them into your home, it can be an open door for demonic visitations.

> *A few years ago I was asked to pray for a man who was being tormented by demons, especially during the night. His wife couldn't sleep in the room with him because he slept with the lights on all night. His little girl would not sleep in her room because in the middle of the night a woman would come into the room with blood running down her face. The mother and daughter slept together every night on the sofa in the den.*
>
> *When he came to my house for prayer, I asked him a lot of questions trying to figure out how the demon spirits were able to interfere in his life. (There always has to be an open door, either by him, his ancestors, or his immediate family.) He answered no to all my questions, so I asked if I could go to his house and look around. He agreed, so I went over there and walked through all the rooms.*
>
> *The last room I went in was his bedroom, and immediately I saw the problem. It was an oriental man (shaman or Tibetan monk) encased under Plexiglas holding a bowl and praying to his god. I told him he needed to get rid of it in order to be free of the spirits tormenting him and his family. Having it in his possession and his attachment to it was an invitation to the demonic. It had been a gift; he also had another object from this same relative in his bedside table. He said he would get rid of it, but as far as I know he never did because of sentimental reasons. The last I heard he was still being tormented.*

Like this man who wouldn't get rid of the things in his possession, your open doors to the enemy can affect other people, especially your family: Adam's sin affected all mankind and Achan's sin affected all of Israel (see Joshua chapter 7).

Pride and rebellion are at the root of most invitations for the demonic.

Ask the Lord to help align your will with His so you will be willing to do whatever is necessary. In 1 Kings 22:13-23 King Ahab allowed himself to be deceived because he wasn't willing to go against his wife, Jezebel; therefore, he couldn't be free from her demonic hold over him, as described in 1 Kings 21:25. He did repent, but later returned to Jezebel's influence over him.

Prayer: *Lord, forgive me for my disobedience, both to You and to my parents even in my youth. I repent of my rebellion. Please search my heart, show me any specific things I need to repent of, and help me to receive Your forgiveness. Show me if there is anyone I need to go to in person to ask forgiveness. Amen.*

> *I have a friend who was into what she called white witchcraft, which was supposed to be used for benevolent purposes. She thought white witchcraft was okay because she wasn't using it to put curses on people. However, it opened the door for her and her "significant other," who later became her husband, to be tormented by a witch who was into serious witchcraft. The Lord used it to get their attention. Fearful, they started looking for someone who had more power and could tell them how to make the manifestations in their home stop. They were told about a local chiropractor, who was supposed to have strong spiritual powers. They made an appointment hoping he could help them, but they soon found out that he had become a Christian. After repenting, they both accepted the Lord and received a greater power themselves. They no longer needed anyone else's help. The Holy Spirit had entered the scene!*

Examples of things to confess, repent and get rid of.

- Things related to the occult or past sin, i.e. jewelry, momentos from someone you had a sinful relationship with, photos. (I'm not talking about all your memories here. Mainly we are referring to things you need to get rid of that take you back and cause wrong desires, or trigger unhealthy memories.)

- It might be things with unknown history, which are not inherently evil, but the Spirit may be telling you that they were associated with evil.

- Anything that has become a god in your life (clothes, jewelry, money, antiques, artifacts).

- Artifacts, books and things honoring Hindu, Bhudda, Edgar Cayce, Jean Dixon, or other prominent modern day soothsayers or false prophets; and material related to Mormonism, Jehovah's Witness, Unity, Scientology, Zen, Freemasonry, Eastern Star.

- Games; art, new age, yoga, pyramids, zodiac, witchcraft, crystals, martial arts, horoscopes, porn, posters, *Harry Potter* and similar type books, good luck charms, rings, yin and yang symbols.

- Things connected to unholy relationships: trinkets, letters, souvenirs, books, stuffed animals, photos, music, jewelry, clothing, furniture, and wall hangings.

- Whatever relates to past sin strengthens the enemy's hold over you. This includes emotional, psychological, physical, or spiritual attachments.

It doesn't hurt to cleanse a home you move into by praying blessings over it. Deal with spiritual ownership if it was not godly. If there was a foreclosure, repent of financial sins of prior owners and break any curse over the home while anointing the doorposts with oil.

Demons are deceptive

Demons operate through people and will act like your friends. Acting as if to minister to your needs because you are vulnerable, they make you think you can count on them, but instead they try to destroy you. It might be through an unhealthy relationship with a person who is allowing the enemy to manipulate him/her, and that person is, in turn, trying to manipulate you or speak deceptions into your life. Examples would be co-dependent relationships, adultery, gossip, bad advice on financial decisions and relationships. Sometimes we rely on our natural coping skills rather than dealing with it as the spiritual problem it is.

God Moment:

Close your eyes and listen . . .

My child, I see your heart and it is to know Me. Let me fill those empty places and comfort you in those places that are raw from past hurts. My desire for you is healing and wholeness. In order to heal, you must be sure to forgive. Then My healing balm will flow freely.

When you are free and know that I don't condemn you and I haven't forsaken you, then the walls will come down, and you will fully open up your heart to Me. I'm here waiting to shelter you under My wings and wrap you in My embrace.

Malachi 4:2; Psalm 61:1-3; Romans 8:1

Assignment:

Make a list of things in your past that you need to repent of and renounce.

_____
_____
_____

In what way do you think demonic powers and principalities have influenced our nation?

_____
_____
_____

Ask God what you might have wrong thinking about.

_____
_____
_____

Final Thought:

Jesus is stronger than any demonic entity, so your faith is in His ability, not yours. He will do for you what you cannot do for yourself by faith through His grace.

Journal:

Lesson 12: Freedom

Steps to freedom: confess, repent, forgive.

Present yourself before the Lord for His inspection. Ask the Lord to open your eyes. Self-evaluation is not enough because the heart is deceitful (Jeremiah 17:9). Ask Christian family members and Godly friends for insight as well.

Sanctify yourself by committing to live for the Lord. Repent of bad attitudes or behavior. Forgive anyone who has offended you.

Do identificational repentance, if needed, in which you stand before the Lord to confess and repent of others' sin that have affected you. Examples of that would be your parents or grandparents who passed down curses through their involvement in things they never repented of — such as addictions, false relgions or occult involvement, etc.

Locate the offensive items and rid yourself of those things that defile (e.g. books, occult games, statues, certain music, and other things related to sin).

Be serious about it, but not paranoid. Renounce the enemy and your association with him. Break any contracts and unholy ties you have made with darkness whether willingly or unwillingly.

Consecrate your life and property to the glory of the Lord.

Prayer: *I break any and all unholy soul ties that were made while in my ungodly relationship with_____. I sever these ties now by the blood of Jesus. In doing so, I take back any ground I gave the enemy by committing that sin. Amen*

Evil spirits get people to believe a lie and then act accordingly. The main reason they want to dominate is to fulfill Satan's desire to direct and manipulate the destiny of man. He has to be anonymous to accomplish his purposes — he wants to steal your identity.

While the term "demon possession" is not mentioned in scripture, it does say "demonized," meaning to be moved upon or within by an unclean spirit or spirits.

Some ways to recognize the enemy at work: Strongholds — strong feelings that take hold.

Blame

- The Lie: You are a victim, or development of a victim mentality, *i.e.*, either *I am to blame for everything*, or, *everyone else is to blame*.
- Followed by thoughts and feelings such as: *it's my fault, I'm no good, I'm depressed, or ashamed*.
- Related actions: you live below your God-given abilities, defensive, with no joy, controlled by lying spirits, and isolated.

Fear

- The Lie: Some version of: *I can't get it right, I am a failure, I don't measure up*
- Followed by thoughts and feelings such as: *I have to be perfect or something bad will happen, efforts alone are not acceptable*, and feelings of anxiety.
- Related actions: you're overly timid, suffer from panic attacks, phobias, and indecision.

Rejection

- The Lie: *If they really get to know me, they won't like me; there is something wrong with me.*
- Followed by thoughts and feelings such as: *I will find comfort in food, alcohol, drugs, sex, pornography, other addictions*.

- Related actions: you withdraw from people, are jealous of those who do "fit in," experience insecurity, and are fearful of making close friends; you're overly timid, always comparing yourself to others.

Confusion

- The Lie: *You can't trust or rely on anyone.*
- Followed by thoughts and feelings such as: being suspicious, skeptical, nervous, feeling in turmoil, exhibiting mental illness, chronic doubt, or unbelief.
- Related actions: excessive nervousness about making decisions, operating from distorted judgment, or trouble praying.

Anger

- Lie: *It's not really my fault.*
- Followed by thoughts and feelings such as: being in denial, anger, which turned inward causes you to be depressed; you have a build-up of bitterness and resentment.
- Related actions: you have explosions of rage when the pressure builds, have trouble forgiving, and a desire for or actually seek revenge.

Pride

- Lie: *I am in control, I don't need anyone else.*
- Followed by thoughts and feelings such as: *I want to be my own god, I think things matter more than people, I feel superior to others, I am impatient with those I feel are inferior.*
- Related actions: you become self-righteous, mocking, sarcastic, secretive; you seek power and position, are materialistic and judgmental.

We must understand that the battle is in the mind first. Spirits work first from the outside trying to get inside. Man is a free moral agent, not a robot. One of the enemy's greatest weapons is *suggestion*. First there will be oppression, then obsession in your mind, and then the spirit gains control over your body. If you are deliberating connecting with the realm of darkness, it could then go down into your spirit, and you could be completely demonized if you are not a believer.

The Holy Spirit works in Christians from the inside out, unholy spirits work from the outside in.

Sometimes the gift of discerning of spirits needs to be in operation before we can effectively minister deliverance to someone. The Holy Spirit can reveal to you what you are dealing with. If most people knew they were cooperating with an evil spirit in the decisions they make, they would rethink how they respond in most situations and circumstances.

Satan still has the power to deceive and corrupt the minds of Christians, but he has even more power over the lost (2 Corinthians 11:3). He blinds the minds of unbelievers (2 Corinthians 4:4). In James 4:7 we are told to resist him and he will flee. People are not going to be protected automatically; we have to work together with God and apply his blood to the situation and repent of any sin or unforgiveness that could have opened the door.

Once you are free, it's important to change your thinking and renew your mind with the Word of God.

Did the early Romans name their deities? In his book, *Storming Hell's Gates,* Dick Bernal says that in his research (he does not give his source), he discovered a fascinating bit of information on how the early Romans named their deities. He said that in certain instances a mysterious voice came out of nowhere to provide the name. The functions of these deities were to be sharply defined, and in approaching them, it was essential to use their proper names and titles. If one knew the name, one could be assured of a "hearing." It's interesting that Jesus asked the name of the ruling demon in the man in Gadara. (See Luke 8:26-40 for the full story.)

Sometimes when you actually name the demonic spirit you are dealing with, the person is able to be freed from the bondage due to the revelation (through the name) of the lie he/she has believed. Blame is an example. If you believe and agree with the lies of the enemy that something is your fault, then you will be in agreement with the devil. That gives him power to control your thinking. It will open you up to a tormenting spirit. Yet if you realize the change and name the spirit of blame in the context of healing prayer, and find that the blame disappears, then you know you were being influenced by the enemy.

See the next workbook in this series, *Healing Prayer,* for more on how to do this.

Healing, deliverance and discernment of spirits work together.

In the early Church, when a person became a believer, he/she was actually expected to go through deliverance. The 7th Council of Carthage in AD 276 by Crescens of Certa says *all heretics and "schismatics" who wish to come to the Catholic Church will not be allowed to enter without they have first been exorcised by water baptism.* Scripture says that demons look for waterless places to find rest (Luke 11:24), so apparently they don't like water. Sometimes people are instantly delivered, or the demons begin to manifest when they are immersed in water through baptism. Missionaries often see this happen in Africa with new converts, due to their occult practices before being saved.

Most people don't realize they are opening doors by what they are doing, and they end up giving Satan an entry into their life.

The following is an example of how you can give Satan an entry into your life by opening a door without realizing you are doing anything:

There was an August 2011 article I read titled, "Wiccan Days Part Of Vandy Calendar." It goes on to say that Wiccan and pagan students at Vanderbilt University might get to take an excused day off from class to dance around the Maypole. They were included in the calendar of 2011-12 "religious holy days and observances." The faith "Wicca/Pagan" was listed next to four of the days on the calendar. Wiccans believe they are worshipping other gods and goddesses, but Satan rules them all. Their views of divinity are generally theistic, and revolve around a goddess great mother (the eternal virgin) and a horned god who is supposed to rule over the after-world paradise, thereby being generally dualistic. I would hope these students would not continue down this path of religion, especially if they knew they were actually worshipping Satan.

Our battle is in the heavenly places.

Although the actual battle may be taking place supernaturally in "heavenly places," it is clear that our earthly, physical actions have a direct impact on that battle. In addition, our spiritual warfare has a supernatural effect on our physical circumstances. A great illustration of this is found in the account of Paul and Silas in the book of Acts. They were unjustly arrested as Jews who were disturbing the peace in the city of Philippi in Macedonia.

The crowd joined in attacking them, and the magistrates tore the garments off them and gave orders to beat them with rods. And when they had inflicted many blows upon them, they threw them into prison (Acts 16:22-23).

The jailor was charged to watch them carefully, and he incarcerated them in a high security cell and fastened their feet in stocks. It was the middle of the night. They were beaten and in pain, isolated and uncomfortable. What were they to do? Paul and Silas started praising God and singing with all their hearts, so loudly that all the prisoners heard them. The whole atmosphere of the place changed. Right there in the dark, dank prison, they were building a throne for the Presence of the King (Psalm 22:3)! Sure enough, the Lord intervened and the situation changed dramatically (Acts 16:26).

Steps to effective healing through deliverance[8].

These steps help bring healing that involves getting to the root instead of just picking the fruit, which will grow back:

The following will help bring healing through getting to the root of the problem (i.e., bad fruit, bad root.) Follow these steps on your journey to healing:

1. Be transparent and humble — be honest about your issues by bringing into the light whatever is hidden in darkness because evil spirits will feed on darkness (Psalm 139:23-24). Let go of pride and allow the Holy Spirit to bring healing through being open with those ministering (James 4:6-7; 5:16a).

2. Repent and renounce — confess your sins 2 Corinthians 7:10, and renouce them, meaning you don't intend to repeat them (Acts 19:18, 19).

---

8 *See Appendix D for more information:*

3. Forgive — sometimes we even need to forgive God as well as others and ourselves (Matthew 18:21-15).

4. Pray — with authority (Joel 2:32).

5. Conduct warfare — when you pray with authority, command by name the tormenting spirits in the name of Jesus to leave (Mark 16:17; Luke 10:19; Psalm 18:2).

Jesus demonstrated the superiority of His kingdom over Satan's in four ways in Mark 1:15-26:

1. Jesus dealt with the demon, not the man. He spoke to the demon. Jesus expelled the demon from the man, not the man from the synagogue.

2. Jesus was not embarrassed by the interruption or disturbance because dealing with demons was part of His ministry.

3. The demon spoke in both singular and plural form when speaking for itself and on behalf of others.

4. The man was a regular member of the synagogue, but nobody knew he had a demon. The anointing probably caused it to manifest.

Jesus became known first as the Man with unique authority over demons when launching His public ministry.

There's more detail about healing prayer in the next workbook, but consider the following a good preview of how to gain victory over what the enemy has stolen or attacked.

Some things to be aware of when praying for a person's freedom.

Sometimes the person's symptoms are the work of an evil spirit or demon. Jesus asked the demon in the man in Mark 5:9 what his name was. This isn't always necessary, but if you don't know what you are dealing with, sometimes a person won't be completely delivered. Evil spirits can be deceptive in a deliverance experience, so check again. They are aware if you are hesitant and if you don't know what you are doing. Affirm to the person that they themselves are in control, not the evil spirit. They know in their heart what they struggle with and what is dominating them, so they can name it and speak to whatever it is and command it to go. They will usually know if they are free and if all the evil spirits have left. Most of the time a person will feel "lighter," and even their countenance will change.

Many times the evil spirit you address will be a symptom as in Mark 9:25 when Jesus rebuked the unclean spirit and commanded the mute and deaf spirit to come out of the boy. To get to the root of the problem, you might ask when they came in and how long they have been there.

Evil spirits have a psyche; they can be encouraged and discouraged. The strongman is the one who brings in the others, and they function under him (Luke 11: 21-22). This one will be the root problem that opened the door.

Jesus is stronger than any demonic entity, so your faith is in His ability, not yours. Evil spirits have a purpose and function and find protection in a community support system. When you break off the main stronghold, the strongman and his kingdom (those who came in as a result of the main bondage/trauma), the person will become free. If the strongman or one in control who opened the door for the others is not identified, then go through others until the main one is found.

The main problem will be emotions that control the person as in pride, self-pity, unforgiveness, fear, or a trauma they've experienced. Some things causing that would be struggles with shame, timidity, inferiority, etc.

Personalize it; they are responsible. Have them participate by having them tell the evil spirit to leave. Deliverance is easier when they speak to the demonic realm and become accountable for their own part in whatever opened the door. Have them confess, repent, and forgive others, themselves, and God.

Remember to look for these responses, verbal and nonverbal, in a person receiving prayer if an evil spirit is manifesting.

1. Sensations in their body or yours when asked a question. This can be nonverbal contact from a demon.
2. Blanking out altogether, not being able to focus.
3. Sight changes in their vision, face, or pain (nonverbal).
4. Thoughts might come to your mind or ask them what comes to their mind. They and you need to just report and not try to interpret.
5. Hear a voice in your head (verbal contact).
6. Speak with authority (don't yell) and tell the person receiving deliverance to use a controlling voice. Instruct them to command, submit, and get involved in resisting the enemy. When dealing with the demonic, it's all about authority.
7. Ask them what they are thinking or feeling.
8. If you think the ministry is done, ask them how they feel. If they feel heaviness, they probably need more prayer. They will usually feel lighter and a sense of relief if they are free.

People usually can tell if they are free.

When spirits leave a person, they usually leave through the nose or mouth. A person might exhale, sigh, yawn, sneeze, cough, or just breathe out. Some might scream, vomit phlegm, or even belch.

Coughing or sighing is the most common. (From this comes the idea of breathing in the Holy Spirit to be filled and to get rid of demons one breathes out.)

Forgiveness is key to deliverance, healing, and staying free.

Have the person confess any sin of rebellion, unforgiveness, etc., and exercise authority over any spirit attached (Psalm 139:19-24; Psalm 103). Take back any ground found in their past, family, or ancestors. Scriptures helpful in warfare: Hebrews 2:14-15, 12:1-15; Ephesians 1:15-22; Galatians 5:16-26; 1 John 5:18; Romans 6, 8:31-39.

God will do for us what we cannot do for ourselves, but He will not do for us what He requires us to do for ourselves. He holds us responsible to exercise scriptural discipline over our own thoughts (1 Thessalonians 5:8). God has provided the helmet of salvation for our hope. He has given us hope to protect our minds (Hebrews 6:18-20). It's up to everyone to walk in his/her new freedom.

Everything in the kingdom of God comes through faith by grace.

Keeping your deliverance:
- Put on the armor of God.
- Stay in the scripture; use only positive confessions about yourself and from the Word. (Your mind is the battleground for demonic influence.)
- Praise, worship, and prayer are important to stay free.
- Fellowship and commitment to follow the Lord.
- It's important to "fill the house." When an evil spirit is cast out, it will try to return (Matthew 12:43-45).

- Since evil spirits are the opposite of the fruit of the Spirit, ask for the Holy Spirit to fill the person with the fruit of the Spirit (Galatians 5:22-23). The fruit of the Spirit represent the nature of Jesus. The "house" has to be filled with Jesus.

You can minister deliverance to yourself, but it is usually helpful to have someone else there. You can also stand in for someone else you believe needs help (Matthew 15:22-28; Acts 19: 11-12). This is a form of intercession but is not the norm. However you choose to intercede, be sure to ask the Lord first; don't be impulsive about it. Read Galatians 5, and be careful about the people you choose to pray for and with you. In many cases, after deliverance, you'll also want to follow up with counseling in order to relearn certain behaviors.[9]

Based on Ephesians 6:1-10, Paul considered the following to be effective in spiritual warfare against the forces of darkness: truth, righteousness, the Gospel, faith, salvation, the Word of God, prayer, and perseverance.

God Moment

Close your eyes and listen . . .

Beloved, don't be afraid of what you don't understand. I am bigger than all of it. Don't be overwhelmed by circumstances. I'm in control when you hand it over to Me and trust Me. I've got your back; don't fear, lean into Me.

Allow Me to handle those things that are too hard and overwhelming for you. Hand Me the burdens you carry for others. They are not meant for you.

---

9 See Appendix D – Points of Note on Deliverance Ministry

My yoke is easy and My burden is light. Be yoked to Me and let Me lead you. I will take you in the direction you need to go.

Matthew 11:30

Galatians 6:2

Assignment:

Would you ever feel confident praying deliverance for someone? Why or why or not?

_____

_____

Do feel you need some deliverance yourself? Why?

_____

_____

What would be different if you did?

_____

_____

Final Thought

Jesus is stronger than any demonic entity, so your faith is in His ability, not yours. He will do for you what you cannot do for yourself by faith through His grace.

Journal:

For Further Study

Michael Heiser: *The Unseen Realm; Demons; The Divine Council*

Caroline Leaf: *Retrain Your Brian; Switch on Your Brain*

Charles Kraft: *Defeating Dark Angels*

David Appleby: *It's Only a Demon*

Derek Prince: *Spiritual Warfare*

Cindy Jacobs: *Possessing the Gates of the Enemy*

Timothy M. Willis: *Yahweh's Elders (Isa 24:23) Senior Officials of the Divine Court*

Watchman Nee: *Spiritual Man*

Dr. Henry Malone: *Shadow Boxing*

J.P. Moreland: *A Simple Guide to Experience Miracles: Instruction and Inspiration for Living Supernaturally in Christ*

David Stern: *Jewish New Testament Commentary*

Walter J. Veith: *Truth Matters*

C.S. Lewis: *The Screwtape Letters*

Timothy Warner: *Spiritual Warfare*

Dick Bernal: *Storming Hell's Gates*

Voddie T. Baucham: *Fault Lines: The Social Justice Movement and Evangelicalism's Looming Catastrophe*

Appendix A: Breaking the Masonic Curse

Always start by making sure that the person has accepted Jesus as his/her Lord and Saviour and understands his/her authority of blood covenant through salvation.

Start by binding specific Freemasonry spirits:

Bind: Death, anti-Christ, deception, lust, sadism or sadistic tendencies, calamity, satan, lies, domination, manipulation, consumption, witchcraft, control and jezebel in Jesus' name.

On the 1st degree only, say:

I bind and cancel the cable toe and hoodwink and spirit of Shiva in Jesus' name.

On the 1st degree through the 27th degree individually; get the person to repeat the following:

I bind and break the power of the spirits of the ___ degree mason and loose them from and cast them far beneath me. I cancel the oaths and curses as if they have never been spoken. I loose from me all the collars and aprons and regalia in Jesus' name.

On the 28th degree through the 33rd degree individually; get them to repeat:

I bind and break the power of the spirit of witchcraft; and I bind and break the power of the spirits of the ___ degree mason and loose them from me and cast them far beneath me. I cancel the oaths and curses as if they have never been spoken. I loose from me all the collars and aprons and regalia in Jesus' name.

1st degree
2nd degree
3rd degree
4th degree
5th degree
6th degree
7th degree
8th degree
9th degree
10th degree
11th degree
12th degree
13th degree
14th degree
15th degree
16th degree
17th degree
18th degree
19th degree
20th degree
21st degree
22nd degree
23rd degree
24th degree
25th degree
26th degree
27th degree
28th degree
29th degree
30th degree
31st degree
32nd degree
33rd degree

Appendix B: Recognizing and Defining Demonic Activity

Ways to recognize demonic influence

1. If you have the gift of discerning of spirits and see or perceive demonic influence, be sure this is not merely suspicion coming from your flesh, but is divinely revealed through the Spirit.

2. Detection — observing what they do to a person. This is not the same as a person mentally struggling with with a temptation, but someone genuinely influenced by something not of themselves. It can include symptions such as:

- Emotional problems
- Mental problems
- Sexual problems
- Addictions
- Physical infirmities
- Religious error, such as involvment in cults, or the occult
- False doctrines championed as real

3. You may recognize repetitive behavior that could signal generational demonic problems, such as:

- Insanity or emotional disturbances
- Hereditary afflictions, such as chronic illness, heart disease, diabetes, etc. that can have natural, lifestyle and spiritual roots
- Difficulties with conception, pregnancy, or other female problems
- Divorce, divisive family relationships
- Persistent financial lack
- Being accident prone
- Suicide or other unnatural premature or violent deaths

Again, you must be discerning to detect demonic influence. Many of the above-mentioned issues can have natural causes, spiritual causes, or both. If they are persistent and don't respond to traditional remedies, it can be worthwhile to investigate a possible spiritual root through healing prayer.

Demonic Definitions

Amulet: an ornament or charm supposedly charged with magical power and used to ward off spells, disease, and bad luck, etc.

Ankh: from Egyptian paganism, a cross with a loop at the top (identified with the goddess Isis) represents in the occult eternal life and the union of male and female. It's used in fertility rites.

Astrology: scriptures calls it "soothsaying" which is a form of divination used to seek information about the past, present, or future through supernatural methods, by revealing hidden meanings in the natural world, or ascribing secret meaning to patterns or images. It is used to chart your life and make decisions by the signs of the Zodiac, horoscope.

Aura: an energy field believed to surround a person's body with different colors revealing the spiritual, psychological and physical state of the person.

Black magic: magic used for harm, deceit, or destruction.

Channeling: when someone allows a spirit (demon) to speak through him/her.

Charm: chanted or spoken words used to invoke a spell, or an object said to have supernatural power. In today's culture what the Bible called charmers or chanters we would refer to as hypnotists. A passive state, as in hypnosis, is dangerous because it leaves the mind unguarded and consequently susceptible to any spirit waiting for an opportunity. Even if you don't have a spirit take over a part of your mind it can hinder the Holy Spirit.

Clairvoyants: psychics who claim to see objects or people who may have been lost. Familiar spirits become their spirit guides. Edgar Cayce is an example of gaining information from a familiar spirit to heal people. These are called "readings." These spirits will lead people into believing in reincarnation.

Cycle: an interval during which a recurring sequence of events happens. It can be a periodically repeated sequence of events, (destructive cycles) something that happens over and over at a certain time. It can be linked with a time or an event and orchestrated supernaturally so that a repeating wound or injustice occurs from generation to generation. It causes us to go around the same mountain.

Demonized: demons inhabit certain areas in a person's emotions, mind and body.

Demons: to occultists they are any non –human spirit. One theory is that they are "fallen angels (Revelation 12:4,7);" second theory is that they are disembodied spirits of the offspring of a superior race creating by co-habitating with female humans Genesis 6:1-6, and theory number three is that they are the "disembodied spirits" of a pre-Adamic race of humans that was so polluted that God was forced to destroy the whole human race and recreate it with Adam (Genesis 1:3, 16, 28). This last one is because God told Adam to replenish the earth. That could be taken to mean to reproduce and replace those who had been destroyed (angels who rebelled against God.)

Divination: the attempt to gain knowledge of people or events by occult means, palm reading fortune telling, Ouiji board, Tarot cards, crystals, tea leaves, horoscopes, etc. It counterfeits the work of the Holy Spirit (Acts 16:16-18). It is linked with familiar spirits.

ESP: abbreviation for people who use extrasensory perception to know or communicate outside of normal methods; includes telepathy (communicating with the mind alone) and clairvoyance (seeing objects or actions apart from the time and space in which they occurred, intuitive knowledge).

Fallen Angels: created beings that rebelled against God and now serve Satan. It's believed they have ranks.

Familial Spirit: is one that leaves one family member and goes to another to express their personality. It can happen at death or when the first inhabitant is no longer receptive. Spirits don't die but people do.

Familiar Spirit: gives information from demonic sources such as mediums and clairvoyants (1 Samuel 28:7-8; Isaiah 8:19). It might be from a deceased person, spirit belonging to the family or familiar with that person. In the Hebrew it means "knowing spirit." They know about you. Ghosts are familiar spirits impersonating real people who have died. They usually include necromancy, mediums, clairvoyance, spiritists, yoga, prophecy, TM, ESP, mind-altering drugs, etc.

Hypnotism: opens you up to wrong spirit realm because you become passive.

Incubus: Wesbster defines incubus as "an evil spirit that lies on persons in their sleep; one that has sexual intercourse while they are sleeping." It takes on the form of a man to sleep with a woman.

Infirmity: sickness and disease or suffering and sorrow that can keep you from standing strong. It can be a disability of some kind. It can occur as a result of moral or spiritual defects that cause our will to stray from God. It can be caused by a demon to keep us from standing strong (Luke 13:11). It can be linked to an overall weakness in our body or with anything that created the weakness, such as grief (Romans 15:1; Romans 8:26). We bear each other's weaknesses in intercession.

Kabbalah: from Judaism, an esoteric system based on the belief that the Torah is a code with four levels of meaning. Men and women are considered broken vessels that must repair themselves to advance spiritually and regain Eden.

Kachina dolls: are believed to be reincarnated humans who have become gods (Indian culture).

Karma: from Hinduism, the law of cause and effect, in which one's actions have consequences in future lives.

Kinds of demons: lying, unclean, divination, deceiving, jealousy, haughtiness, seducing, infirmity, heaviness, deaf and dumb, fear; death; anti-Christ, error, perverse, bondage, etc.

Magic: the attempt to influence or control people or events by occult means including black and white magic.

Materialization: the physical manifestation of a spirit being.

Medium: a psychic who attempts to communicate with the dead.

Necromancy: communication with the supposed spirits of the dead.

Obsession: this level of demonic activity begins to affect the mind as well as the function of a person.

Occult: the word means "to conceal or cause to disappear from view – to be secret or hidden, mysterious, supernatural." It can refer to secret or hidden knowledge available to initiates, the supernatural, and the parapsychology and paranormal phenomena.

Oppression: demonic activity from the outside involving temptation or harassment.

Pantheism: the belief that God and creation are essentially one, and that the universe and its inhabitants share in God's divine nature.

Pentagram: a five-pointed star formed by five straight lines, usually placed within a circle. Used as a symbol and in rituals by Wicca and most Witchcraft. Satanists use an inverted pentagram with two points turned upward.

Polytheism: the belief in many gods.

Possession: being demonized from the inside where the demons have control.

Psychic: a person who receives information through spirits or supernatural abilities.

Psychometric: holding an object belonging to someone else and gaining knowledge about him or her.

Satan: the adversary, chief of the rebellion against God. Satan worshipers believe he is more powerful than God and will reward them, or that he is an angel of wisdom who was mistreated by an evil God. The most popular group believes he is not a personal being but a symbol representing rebellion against God and the morals of society. They believe he symbolizes being your own God. They revere the carnal self and self-indulgence.

Séance: a gathering at which people attempt to contact the dead.

Sorcery: magic, usually of the black variety. The use of spirits or drugs to access supernatural power, sometimes considered by occultists to be the use of harmful or black magic.

Spiritualism: contact the dead or spirits.

Spirit guide: a spirit being that acts as one's guide, commonly found in the occult and New Age.

Succubus: Webster defines succubus as "a demon that takes on a female form in order to have sexual intercourse with men while they are asleep."

Telekinesis: controlling objects with the mind.

Third eye: from Hinduism, one of the chakras (invisible energy centers) located between the eyes that bestow psychic powers.

Totems: a Thunderbird, messenger of Satan, believed to be a god patrolling the heavens.

Transcendental Meditation (TM): the repetition of a special word uttered over and over again to attain relaxation and other benefits.

Voodoo: an occultist religion that combines magic, spiritism, and the use of fetishes.

White Magic: magic that is supposedly helpful or beneficial. It's usually done through visualization, incantations, and/or magical tools. Some defend it as doing good but reject "black" magic as doing harm.

Wicca: a witch who mainly worships a variety of gods and goddesses. They don't believe in a being called Satan so they don't worship him. Follow the Wiccan Rede, which says to "Do no harm, and do what you will." They revere nature. Many witches and wiccans see no difference between prayer and casting spells because they think both are invoking a power to fulfill one's desire. Includes a group called "Goths."

Witches: one who is usually credited with malignant supernatural powers; to influence or beguile with wile and charm; to affect injuriously with witchcraft.

For scriptural references, see:

Exodus 20:5; Deuteronomy 4:15-19, 23-32, 39-40; 5:7-9; 6:1-18; 7:11-13, 26; Deuteronomy 22:5; 23:14; Chronicles 7:14; Joshua 7:11-13; Psalm 115:1-8; Isaiah 1:4-15, 8:19; 2; Jeremiah 10:1-8, 10-15, 23-25; Amos 5:26; Habakkuk 2:18-19 (Amp); Acts 19:19; Romans 1:17-32

Open Doors for Demonic Entry

Inherited Curses

Some demons apparently come down the family line. They often manifest after birth. It is suspected that they are present even as the child is being formed. This seems particularly true of the demons of:

They are able to enter at this early age because of the "legal ground" from Sins of the Fathers (and mothers).

Another form of "inheritance" occurs when one or more of our ancestors have dedicated or committed their descendants to their particular god or occult guild (i.e. witchcraft, freemasonry). Here, the demons claim "ownership" right from the womb and will do all within their power to prevent the person from hearing or understanding the Gospel.

The good news is that the Blood of Jesus overrides and neutralizes any other blood that has ever been shed.

Sins of the Flesh

These sins are the "door" that we most frequently open to invite the enemy in to destroy us. This is especially true when the sin is repeated and becomes a pattern, leading to a lifestyle of indulging the flesh.

These are the common areas in which we indulge our carnal appetites:

Anger

Fear

Greed/Covetousness

Jealousy/Envy

Rebellion

Pride   1 Timothy 3:6-7; Ezekiel 28:12-19

Lust

Gluttony

Gossip

Strife

165

Bitterness

Self-Righteousness

Criticizing, Blaming, Judging

Unforgiveness

Illness and Accidents

Illness provides an opportunity for demons to enter. Defenses are lowered, the will is weakened, and the ability to pray for oneself is lessened. Demons love to take advantage of our vulnerability and to kick us when we are down.

With illnesses, we have the added liability of medical drug use. Anything that we are in bondage to is a potential open door for Demonic Oppression.

Emotional Trauma

A traumatic emotional or physical experience fractures the defenses that normally keep demons out.

Common examples are:

- Breakup of a relationship
- Divorce
- Unexpected death
- Job loss
- Abuse

Other more severe forms include:

- Violence
- Rape
- Ritual sexual abuse

When any of these occur in childhood, it can lead to fractured or multiple personalities as part of our "coping" mechanism for survival.

Passive or Trance State of Mind

When one gives up his will in a passive or trance state of mind. The person may become partially or even completely controlled by the demonic.

Three main ways that we allow our minds to enter the passive state that will make us vulnerable:

- Trances
- Induced Mental States

- Drugs
- Chants
- Music
- Meditation (yoga or TV)
- Anesthesia

The experience of being anesthetized leaves the mind unguarded.

A strong prayer covering can be very helpful, if not essential, when a person's mind is passive because of anesthesia.

Occult Involvement

This is the major form of idolatry. The word "occult" means "hidden." Occult involvement means looking for knowledge and/or power in "hidden" sources, sources other than the true and living God.

God hates the occult. This is clear through many scriptures:

Deuteronomy 4:19, 18:10-12   Galatians 5:20

Leviticus 20:2-5, 20:6   Revelations 12:8

Appendix C: Angels, Demons, and Sons of God

Not all divine beings are angels. If we closely examine our English language scriptures, along with Aramaic, Hebrew, and Greek, then trace the translations through the years, we can glean fascinating information about the spiritual world. In the ancient Semitic world, the term "sons of God" (in Hebrew, *beny elohim*), was a plural phrase used to identify divine beings with higher-level responsibilities or jurisdictions. We see this same description used outside the Bible in ancient texts from the biblical world. It is also used in Job 1:6. In Job 38, they are also referred to as "morning stars." So, in general, we see that God created both a human and divine family; on the spiritual side, there were (or are) divine beings, sons of God, more literally translated "little gods" that likely witnessed earth's creation (Job 38:7), and serve as God's representatives, just as we are to do here on earth (2 Corinthians 5:20). These divine beings were not referred to as "angels" until the Greek translation of the Hebrew Bible. (For more on this, check out Michael Heiser's book, *The Unseen Realm*.)

You may have heard the term "elohim" used to refer to God. The Old Testament writers seemed to understand that there were many gods (i.e., sons of God, elohim) but only one YAHWEH Elohim, the one true God. Incidentally, the suffix "-im" is what makes elohim plural.

1 Kings 22:19-23 describes a divine council meeting, which we can assume was made up of the Trinity and the elohim. Psalms 82:1 and 89:6-7 talk about the divine council of heavenly beings, presided over by God. You'll also see it mentioned in Daniel 4:13-23.

The concept of a heavenly council was a commonly understood motif in ancient times (Zechariah 3, and Jeremiah 23:18-22); because some of them eventually became corrupt, 1 Corinthians 6:3 says we will judge angels.

Going back to the creation story, the Garden may well have been God's headquarters or throne room here on earth, and the place His heavenly council met. Ezekiel 28 says Eden is the seat of the gods, the seat of governmental authority. If this is true, then it's certainly no coincidence that the Bible ends with the vision of a new Eden-like earth (Revelation 21-22).

In Genesis 3, one of the heavenly council beings presented himself to Eve as a serpent and deceived her. She wasn't surprised or afraid when he began speaking to her, so we can surmise that his presence in the Garden was routine. In Ezekiel 28:14, this being is called a "guardian cherub." This comes from the Hebrew *Kerub* or in Akkadian, *Keribu*, a term meaning a throne guardian. The Akkadian empire was one of the first recognized civilizations in ancient Mesopotamia.

Many assume the rebellion among the elohim happened before creation, or certainly before the Fall of Man; however, many scholars believe the two "Falls" happened simultaneously in the Garden, with the deception involving Adam and Eve — that this was when Satan first sinned by choosing to put his throne above God's (Ezekiel 28; Isaiah 14). He was cast down to earth (*eres*), which was also known as the realm of the dead (Jonah 2:6; Jeremiah 17:13; Psalms 71:20).

Scripture doesn't specifically say that Satan rebelled before Genesis 3. The only scriptural reference to his taking a third of the angels with him in his rebellion is in Revelation 12, which seems to indicate it coincided with the first coming of the Messiah. However, in Luke 10:18, just after the 70 disciples had been sent out to evangelize and prepare the way for his arrival in Jerusalem, Jesus said that He saw Satan fall like lightning from heaven. Was He seeing into the future, or speaking of the past? Read 1 Corinthians 2:6-8 and then decide for yourself. The truth is, we just don't know for certain. You'll find solid Biblical scholars on both sides of this issue.

Corruption: Nephilim, Giants, and Babel

Too often, we skip over scriptures we don't understand, or that seem to challenge our view of the world. I would say one of those frequently skipped-over verses would be Genesis 6:1-4. In the ESV it reads:

> When man began to multiply on the face of the land and daughters were born to them, the sons of God saw that the daughters of man were attractive. And they took as their wives any they chose. Then the LORD said, "My Spirit shall not abide in man forever, for he is flesh: his days shall be 120 years." The Nephilim were on the earth in those days, and also afterward, when the sons of God came in to the daughters of man and they bore children to them. These were the mighty men who were of old, the men of renown.

What this is saying, according to multiple scholars who know far more than I, is that some of the spiritual sons of God left their original God-given assignments and boundaries, came down to earth, and had intercourse with the women (daughters of man) here. Their resulting offspring were the Nephilim, or giants. 2 Peter 2:1-10, and Jude 5-7 refer to their punishment. Clearly, from stories like this and others, celestial beings, whether good or evil, can interact with us by taking human form. In Psalms 82:6-7, we read that God is judging the elohim for corruption and sentences them to forfeit their immortality and die like humans. Revelation 12:13 says war was the result.

After the Genesis 6 corruption of the human race, God brought the great flood. But the corruption wasn't stopped, as we discovered in the workbook text (see page 92 and following).

Nimrod, the grandson of Noah, rose to heights of both leadership and corruption in Babylon, and was connected to Mesopotamian gods and goddesses in Assyria and Babylon. He is credited with being instrumental in building the Tower of Babel; it was the beginning of his kingdom (Genesis 10:8-10). With the attempt to build such a tower, God stepped in and dispersed the nations; He disinherited them and put each nation under the rule of lesser gods, or elohim (Deuteronomy 32:8). There were 70 nations at that time. It's interesting to note that Moses had 70 elders judging the people under him, and in Luke 10, Jesus appointed 70 disciples to go out in pairs to evangelize. So we see the number 70 quite a bit in scripture, when it comes to judging and reigning.

The elohim that had been placed in charge of the nations became corrupt, and embraced the worship that should have gone to YAHWEH Elohim. That's when God called Abraham (then Abram) out of Mesopotamia to be His, from whom would come God's chosen people, the nation of Israel. They were to be a Kingdom of priests that would serve as a conduit for the other nations to return to the One True God (Matthew 22:1-14). This is why you hear the phrase, "Israel is the Lord's portion, and Jacob His inheritance," and why He considered the land of Israel to be holy ground (Deuteronomy 32:9).

Angels and Demons

The New Testament is silent on the exact origin of demons, but the Book of Enoch,[1] asserts that demons are the spirits of the dead Nephilim, from the Genesis 6:1-4 rebellion, wherein some of the sons of God, who were created to be immortal, came to earth and procreated with women here. Their offspring were giants. God passed judgement on their sin, and they were confined to earth, no longer immortal. They are also referred to as "Watcher" spirits of the giant Nephilim.

In Jude 6-7 and 2 Peter 2:4-5, we see that the angels who rebelled are sent into hell, but possibly the spirits of their offspring remain on the earth after death. The truth is, we just don't know for certain.

Just as there are many names for God, from which we can learn about His role in our lives, and promises to us (i.e., Father, Shepherd, Savior, Friend, Almighty, Lion, Lamb, etc.), there are many names that refer to Satan that similarly are designed to inform and teach us about his characteristics:

- Dragon – serpent, Genesis 3:1, Revelation 12:9
- King – his kingdom is in the second heaven, Revelation 9:11
- Ruler of demons – Matthew 12:24
- Devil – slanderer, Matthew 4:1
- Murderer and oppressor, John 8:44, Acts 10:38
- Roaring lion, 1 Peter 5:8
- Tempter (Matthew 4:3) New Age practitioners think they are "enlightened" and Christians are ignorant. Satan was originally an Archangel called Lucifer, "light bearer," after he tried to usurp God's place of dominion and authority he became Satan, "adversary." When we have a desire that is legitimate and God-given, he will try to twist and warp it by influencing how it is directed and used. He wants that desire to control us instead of us submitting it to God to bring it about as He has purposed for our life. Satan will cause it to become our idol and identity, so that instead of having drive, we are driven.
- Wolf (John 10:12) Satan will try to torment you, sabotage relationships (especially those that are God-ordained) through offenses, and thereby abort the plans God has for you. He wants to separate you from the flock.
- Apollyon – Satan's Greek name, as well as Abaddan, the destroyer (Revelation 9:11). He wants to prevent our destiny and destroy nations and individuals.

Angels, too, have their names and associated ranks, which we have discussed elsewhere. Regardless of what they are called, all are messengers for God, and sometimes take on physical form. We see this throughout the Bible.

The archangel Gabriel interprets the vision for Daniel, and gives him understanding (Daniel 8).

Gabriel told Zachariah he would be the father of John the Baptist (Luke 1:11-20).

---

1 The Book of Enoch, also called 1 Enoch, is an ancient Hebrew apocalyptic text thought to have been written by Enoch, Noah's great-grandfather; fragments of it were found among the Dead Sea Scrolls, so it was certainly known to the Jewish and early Christian writers at the time.

Gabriel told Mary that she would give birth to the Messiah (Luke 1:26-38).

An angel (likely Gabriel) visited Samson's mother in Judges 13:3.

Angels appeared to Abraham in Genesis 18.

An angel appeared to Cornelius in Acts 10.

Angels minister to believers, in addition to bringing them communications from God. Minister, in Greek, "leitourges," literally means "servant" especially as in religious duties, like a priest (Romans 13:6, 15:16; Philippians 2:25; Hebrews 1:14; Isaiah 63:9). We see angels ministering by giving guidance to Phillip, Cornelius, and Peter in Matthew 1:20-21, Acts 8:26, 10:1-8, and 11:13-14. They provided for God's people in Genesis 21:17-20; Psalms 78:23-25; and 1 Kings 16:5-7. They are agents of answered prayer, as seen in Daniel 9:2-24; 10:10-12; Acts 12:1-17; and Revelation 8:2-4. And they ministered to Jesus after His forty-day fast in the wilderness following temptation by Satan in Matthew 4:11.

In Summary

Jesus came to redeem mankind and commissioned us to evangelize the nations. Through us He will reclaim those He disinherited and restore what the enemy took from them as a result of the sons of God becoming corrupt. After we have accomplished our commission to evangelize the nations, the fullness of the Gentiles, Israel will be restored and Jesus will return (Romans 9:6-8, 27-28). In the meantime, a host of spiritual beings, both good and evil, interact with us to support or try to thwart our mission.

Appendix D: Points of Note on Healing Prayer/Deliverance Ministry

1. Demons are evil spirits, unclean spirits, and disembodied spirit beings that have an intense desire to occupy a physical body.
2. Matthew 12:28 shows the existence of two opposing kingdoms: the kingdom of God and the kingdom of Satan; it demonstrates the victory of God's kingdom.
3. New Testament evangelism includes casting out demons; scripture does not separate one from the other.
4. Fear of demons comes from demons themselves.
5. Original Greek indicates two distinct entities: daimonion occurs sixty times in the gospels, Acts and Revelation; daimon occurs only once in Matthew 8:31; unclean spirit is used about twenty times in Luke, Acts and Revelation; evil spirit is used six times in Luke and Acts. Greek word for devil is diabolos meaning "slanderer."
6. Satan's primary action is to defame a person's character, especially Christians.
7. The Greek noun daimon gives rise to a verb daimonizo which occurs about twelve times in the New Testatment and in the English translation is "demonize" which means to be influenced by demons, not to be possessed. The Greek word daimonizo conveys no suggestion of ownership, but it means "to subject to demonic influence."
8. Christians can be subjected to demonic influence.
9. Jesus demonstrated the superiority of His kingdom over Satan's in six ways in Mark 1:15:
    - Jesus dealt with the demon, not the man, He spoke to the demon.
    - Jesus expelled the demon from the man, not the man from the synagogue.
    - Jesus was not embarrassed by the interruption or disturbance because dealing with demons was part of His ministry.
    - The demon spoke in both singular and plural form speaking for itself and on behalf of others.
    - Man was a regular member of the synagogue but nobody knew he had a demon. The anointing caused it to manifest.
    - Jesus became known first as the Man with unique authority over demons launching His public ministry.
10. People needing help were normal, respectable, religious people.
11. Twelve disciples were given a twofold impartation of authority: first, to expel demons and second, to heal every kind of sickness (Matthew 10:7-8).

12. After Jesus' death and resurrection, He again commissioned the disciples to cast out demons in His name and that they would speak with new tongues (Mark 16:1).

13. God will do for us what we cannot do for ourselves, but he will not do for us what He requires us to do for ourselves. He holds us responsible to exercise scriptural discipline over our own thoughts (1 Thessalonians 5:8).

14. God has provided the helmet of salvation for our hope. He has given us hope to protect our minds (Hebrews 6:18-20).

15. Our mind is the battleground for the demonic influence that would form strongholds and take us captive. We must come into agreement with the Word of God and not the lies we hear in our head.

16. Negative thoughts and accusations against others and us are from the devil, and must be countered with positive words from Scripture.

17. Praise and thanksgiving is important to stop the attack of the enemy.

18. First, is the reality of demons; second, is the supernatural provision God has given us through deliverance; third, is the need to maintain that deliverance through disciplined application of Scripture.

19. Freedom from the demonic often depends on the willingness of the person to repent of sin.

20. A person must look only to Jesus as the Deliverer.

21. Your appeal must not be based on your good works, but only on the work of the cross – faith and grace.
    - Make sure there is no unforgiveness.
    - Full deliverance is sometimes progressive.
    - Satan's primary weapon against us is guilt, accusing us.
    - Our authority is from the cross and shed blood of Jesus.
    - Two main barriers to deliverance are unforgiveness and resentment.
    - Many problems with demons begin in childhood.

22. Persistent or intractable problems with demons are almost always rooted in the occult.

23. God releases the power of Holy Spirit through us only in the measure that we are victorious in our spiritual conflict with Satan.

24. Demons have no bodies but have normally accepted marks of personality: will, emotion, intellect, self-awareness, ability to speak.

25. Their origin is unclear: fallen angels associated with Satan or disembodied spirits of a pre-Adamic race that perished under the judgment of God

26. Demons or *daimonions* are earthbound while two categories of *theos* and *daimons* are in the heavens (principalities and powers).

27. Lists of demons in scripture: **Old Testament:** jealousy Numbers 5:14,30; ill will/evil Jude 9:23; distressing/evil 1 Samuel 16:14-23, 18:10, 19:9; 2 Chronicles 18:20-22; lying/deceiving 1 Kings 22:22; 2 Chronicles 18:20-22; perverse/distortion/ dizziness Isaiah 19:14; deep sleep Isaiah 29:10; heaviness/fainting/despair Isaiah 61:3; harlotry/prostitution Hosea 4:12-5:4; unclean/impurity Zechariah 13:2; **New Testament:** mute/robbed of speech Mark 9:17; deaf and dumb/deaf and mute Mark 9:25; infirmity/causing sickness/crippling Luke 13:11; divination/predicting the future Acts 16:16; deceiving/deceitful 1 Timothy 4:1; fear/timidity 2 Timothy 1:7; error/falsehood 1 John 4:6.

28.. Other names of demons that may be causing physical infirmity: arthritis, asthma, cancer, crippling, epilepsy, migraine, head pain, sinusitis, and thrombosis.

29. Names of demons in more general areas: adultery, criticism, envy, gossip, hopelessness, murder, rebellion, religion, stress, violence, claustrophobia, disappointment, fantasy, hatred, masturbation, perversion, rejection, self-pity, suicide, witchcraft, shame, mockery, succubus, incubus.

30. Main two spiritual problems: sin and demons.

31. Satan will always attack the weakest point and in the weakest moment.

32. Satan is a legal expert. He looks for any open door by a Christian.

33. Word occult means "covered over" or "concealed."

34. Python spirit is spirit of divination.

35. Psychics' prediction will actually place a curse on the person who receives and believes it.

36. Qualifies as false religions: acknowledges a plurality of gods, practices idol worship in any form, teaches that human beings can ultimately become gods, teaching that people achieve righteousness by own efforts, offering some form of esoteric knowledge available only to a privileged few. (Mormons/Masonry).

37. Witchcraft is universal, primeval religion of fallen man (rebellion/control)

38. Four main aims of witchcraft:
    - To propitiate a higher spiritual being, often regarded as a capricious or malevolent
    - To control the forces of nature, such as rain or good weather for harvest
    - To ward off sickness and infertility, as in Africa, where almost every barren woman goes to the witch doctor for a potion or charm
    - To control other human beings – to terrify enemies in battle or to produce sexual desire in one person toward another.

39. Four levels of modern witchcraft:
    - Open, public, "respectable"
    - "Underground" covens
    - Disguised within society and the Church: rock music, new age cults
    - A work of the flesh, sinful nature manifesting in manipulation, intimidation, domination by using guilt, rage or violence to control another person.

40. Three main purposes of demons: to afflict and torment us; to keep us from knowing Christ as Savior; and to keep us from serving Christ effectively.

41. Demons entice (to sin/do evil), harass (feed on weaknesses), torture (unforgiveness), compel (compulsiveness – gluttony, nail biting, cleaning), enslave (sexual sins), addictions (anything a person has been brought under that is not helpful), defile (thoughts and imaginations), deceive (spiritual manifestations, attack physical body (sickness and disease/spirit of death).

42. Human personality is effected by: negative emotions and attitudes, the mind in doubt, unbelief, confusion, insanity, indecision, compromise, humanism; the tongue by gossiping, lying, exaggeration, criticism, slander; sexual impurity and perversions; physical appetites in eating and drinking, homosexuality.

43. Personal deliverance: affirm your faith in Christ as son of God who died on cross; humble yourself (renounce pride), confess any known sin, repent of all sins, forgive, renounce the every occult and false religion, prepare to be released from every curse placed over your life, take your stand with God by acknowledging that Jesus died to set you free and expel the demons by commanding them to go in the name of Jesus.

44. Keep your deliverance by: live by Word of God, put on garment of praise, discipline, cultivate right fellowship, be filled with the Holy Spirit, water baptism, whole armor of God.

45. Some are not delivered because: no repentance, not desperate, wrong motives (quick fix), desire for attention, not renounced the occult, soulish relationships (want to control), under a curse, sin, need prayer and fasting.

46. Keys to effectiveness: be under authority, two by two, do not minister alone to opposite sex, use cross, blood of Jesus, and Word (sword of Spirit).

47. Manifestations of deliverance might be: mouth by sighing, yawning, screaming, vomiting, gagging, choking, etc. (sometimes people need help expelling demon by coughing)

48. Don't allow Satan to put fear on you. Jesus overcame him by blood of cross.